Letters

to

My Grandkids

Sharing God's Stories
from the book of Genesis

To Lauani Blessing 2·20·22 Dr. Sy

DR. SYLVIA GALVEZ

ISBN 978-1-63961-460-8 (paperback)
ISBN 978-1-63961-461-5 (digital)

Christian Faith Publishing, Inc.
832 Park Avenue
Meadville, PA 16335
www.christianfaithpublishing.com

Printed in the United States of America

I dedicate this book to my grandkids, great-grandkids, and step-grandkids, to the Perez, Galvez, and Cawthorne families, to my loving sister Hortencia Galvez who is with the Lord. She fought ovarian cancer for seven years! And to my sister-in-law, Edythe, who put up a fight with pancreatic cancer; and brother-in-law, John Cawthorne, who died happily.

A special thanks to my Lord Jesus Christ, who said, "Get up and write the letters to your grandkids."

Contents

Preface

On Monday, July 23, 2018, at 3:00 a.m., I was in bed thinking about fasting. I felt like my prayers were not getting answered, and I knew if I were to fast, it would bring me closer to God! "'Even now,' declares the Lord, 'Return to me with all your hearts, with fasting and weeping and mourning'" (Joel 2:12).

I wanted God to speak to me. I wanted validations. I wanted to know if he was listening to me. Then all of a sudden, the Holy Spirit said, "Get up and go write your letters to your grandkids." At that moment, I jumped out of bed, warmed up some water for coffee, and went into my office and began writing. I was so happy that the Holy Spirit gave me the title to this book!

Sweethearts, these letters in this book are descriptions of the stories in the book of Genesis. There are fifty chapters in Genesis. I have interpreted the stories in my own words. Each Bible verse is connected to others, and part of my goal is to help you understand what is going on in the stories. In 2014, I began to study and researched in-depth the Old Testament and the New Testament. I read different Bibles, Life Applications Bibles, Bible study guides, and Bible commentaries. I listened to theological scholars and read books from other authors who wrote stories of the Bible. I listened to my pastor and watched movies regarding the stories in the Bible. I taught the first five books of the Old Testament to Joyce Sander, a good friend, and my grandkids for one year. After educating myself regarding God's word, I realized the stories in Genesis are life lessons because they are happening in our world today. Therefore, I will only focus on the book of Genesis, the first book in the Old Testament.

These stories helped me understand God's love for people. In these letters, you will find people experiencing happy and sad times, brothers killing each other, parents favoring one child over another. Children are deceiving their parents. Luke shares in chapter 12, verses 51 to 53 how there will be no peace between family members but division. "Do you think I came to bring peace on earth? No, I tell you, but division. There will be five in one family divided against each other, three against two, and two against three. They will be division, father against son and son against father, mother against daughter and daughter against mother, mother-in-law against daughter-in-law and daughter-in-law against mother-in-law." We live in a world with evil people. I want you to know what happened during our ancestors' times and how family separation is nothing new. It is currently happening today in our families like it did in Adam's, Eve's, Moses's, Abraham's, Isaac's, and Jacob's days. The only thing that has changed is the time and people.

Deuteronomy 28:15 tells us that people will receive consequences because they refused to love one another and obey God's word. In these letters, I will share stories of how God listened to people and answered their prayers. God is a giving Lord who wants the best for all of us. Unfortunately, in the book of Genesis, many people refuse to listen and love one another. There are clear examples of what happened to them when they chose to live in sin and refused to walk in love.

The same things that took place in the book of Genesis are happening right now in our families!

> People will be lovers of themselves, lovers of
> money, boastful, proud, abusive, disobedient to
> their parents, ungrateful, unholy, without love,
> unforgiving, slanderous, without self-control,
> brutal, not lovers of the good, lovers of pleasure
> rather than lovers of God. (2 Timothy 3:1–4)

People are hurting inside and out. The devil is real and swiping people off their feet to live a sinful life (Job 1:6–7). "There will be terrible times in the last days" (2 Timothy 3:1). I am hoping these chapter letters will bring light to your life, to teach you and help you think before you react to life problems and situations. We do not have to be like our forefathers. God is giving us heads-up through the stories in the book of Genesis. We have the power to change our situation before it is too late.

I think what is so fascinating is how God planned and designed his world. In the book of Genesis, you will read about how God created the earth, humans, animals, trees, plants, oceans, and seas. God chose specific people in the Bible to share his messages. They were people like me, you, with families and friends. We are all called to know God, but only a few of us are chosen to do God's specific work in this world. "For many are invited, but few are chosen" (Matthew 22:13).

God wants us to love our families and neighbors as ourselves. Neighbors can be your friends, the man in the line at the grocery store, your teachers, and any human being. We must love our Lord with all our hearts and with all our minds and with all your strength. "Love your neighbor as yourself. There is no commandment greater than these" (Mark 12:30–31).

People interrupted the Bible in many ways. Interruptions come from life experiences, education, and cultural background. If you disagree, look up the verses in your Bible and find out the truth. I encourage you to have your Bible while you are reading these chapter letters to follow along.

There are sixty-six books in the Bible, thirty-nine in the Old Testament, and twenty-seven in the New Testament (NIV, 1990). An important note to remember, "The Old Testament is in the New Testament revealed, and the New Testament is in the Old Testament concealed" (Saint Augustine, 1887). Forty authors wrote the Bible, and they did not even know each other. There were four hundred years of silence before the New Testament was written. Could you imagine what God was thinking during that quiet time? Four hundred years to us is a long time, but there is no time with God. He created it before he put time on earth.

It has always been a dream for me to write about the stories in the book of Genesis. I want you to know and love God with all your heart. Fear and trust his word. Love people and walk by faith. God guarantees through his word that he will take care of you. "Trust in the Lord with all your hearts and lean not on your understanding; in all your ways acknowledge him, and he will make your path straight" (Proverbs 3:5–6).

When you read these chapter letters, read them with an open heart and mind. Listen to God speak to you. I hope you learn about God in the process because he loves you. He is real. He hears and answers prayers.

In the Old Testament, people did not have access to God like we do today. God chose people and prophets to share his messages. For example, Abraham was the first prophet mentioned in the Bible. "Now return the man's wife, for he is a prophet, and he will pray for you, and you will live" (Genesis 20:7). God instructed prophets and others on what to do and how to speak. The book of Hebrews, chapter 1, tells us, "In the past, God spoke to our forefathers through the prophets at many times and in various ways." Whereas, in the New Testament, we have direct access to our Lord Jesus Christ. All we must do is "ask and it will be given to you; seek, and you will find; knock, and the doors will be open to you" (Matthew 7:7).

May God bless you and open your mind and heart while you read the stories in the book of Genesis. I love you, my precious grandkids and great-grandkids. May God always keep you safe.

Love, Grandma!

Acknowledgment

I want to thank my heavenly Father, who gave me the desire to write the stories in the book of Genesis. Furthermore, I want to thank God for giving me the title to this book. I know you are a powerful God who has control of my life and the world. I am a woman after your heart!

I want to thank my best friend, mentor, and my husband, Herbert L. Cawthorne. When God was handing out husbands, he knew which one to give me. I am forever blessed and thankful to have you as my partner in this life. I love you!

I want to thank my mother, Josie; father, Oscar; and stepmother, Belia, who finally learned to believe in me after all my mistakes in life. Thank you for teaching me to work hard and not give up. Mom, thank you for taking me to church at a very young age so that I could know the word of God! I love you all.

I want to thank my three sons and stepkids who allowed me to share my love and time with hurting foster girls and others who were hurting emotionally. Thank you for caring for your children and teaching them the importance of knowing God's word. I am immensely proud of you Marvin, Mario, Brandy, John, Elise, and Alena. I love you.

Lastly, I want to thank my grandkids and great-grandkids for allowing me to teach you about the word of God. Always remember to put God first in everything you do and stay in prayer. Remember, the devil is real. Rebuke him and always keep your armor on. So to Natalie, Mario, Daniel, Gabriel, Christian, Julissa, Marvin, John, Sylvia, Tony, Azaria, Amay, Benjamin, Alina, Alayna, Trent, Micah, Nayomi, and Mia and to my great-grandkids, Sierra and Joaquin, I love you all so much! God put it in my heart to write these letters to you. They are stories from the book of Genesis that depict life situations that keep families separated because of sin. Sin will keep you separated from God. Anything that keeps you away from God is a sin. There are nineteen grandkids and two great-grandkids. So stay close to each other and keep in touch. Do not fight among each other and let the devil win! Do what Jesus would want you to do. Love one another and others constantly!

Love,
Grandma

The Bible

Greetings, I hope all is well with you. I want to share how there were once Bibles in public schools, and teachers prayed with their students. All that changed on June 17, 1963. The Supreme Court ruled out public school prayers and Bible reading (*Culture War*, 2018). According to some Christian scholars, since then, the following has increased:

1) Divorce rates
2) Teenage pregnancies
3) Abortions
4) Single parents
5) Children born without dads
6) Teen suicides
7) High school dropouts
8) Depression
9) Anger problems
10) Drug and alcohol abuse
11) Crime rate
12) Homosexuality
13) Atheism
14) Christians attending church less

This list can go on and on. Prayer and Bible reading in public schools was a way to keep juvenile delinquency down. The goal was to instill morals, values, and spiritual training. But I honestly believe God allowed this to happen because he gives us free will, free will to make our own decision. Nine men sitting in the Supreme Court decided to outlaw school praying and Bible reading in schools.

Parents who did not believe in God complained that they did not want their kids to be restricted to a religious culture. Therefore, religion is banned from schools. Prayer and Bible reading should start at home! Our parents are the first teachers in our lives. Teach your kids and make sure they have a relationship with God and know his word.

The Bible was first written in the Hebrew language in 1400 BC (Before Christ) and a few Arabic passages. The second time was in Greek; third, in Latin; and fourth, in English. The first human author to write the Bible was Moses. God instructed Moses, "Write down these words, for in following with these words I have made a covenant with you and Israel" (Exodus 34:27). It was the tenth commandment written in the Hebrew language.

Moses is the author of the first five books of the Old Testament. You may hear people call the first five books in the Bible as the Torah, Pentateuch, Mosaic Law, the first five books of the Hebrew text, or the Book of the Law. I like to call it the first five books of Moses or the Torah. Throughout the reading, I will refer to each chapter as chapter letters. My goal is to share the stories and point out the behaviors of the people God chose. I want you to understand how much God loves you and how he created the world. It is history and real-life stories in the book of Genesis. The book of Genesis is the platform for our Lord Jesus Christ, its history repeating itself.

God has plans for everyone on earth if they believe and trust in his word. "'For I know the plan I have for you,' says the Lord. 'They are plans for good and not for disaster, to give you a future and a hope'" (Jeremiah 29:11). Thus, all God wants us to do is love one another and treat people with kindness. Do not hate! It is a sin to be angry and hateful toward your brothers and sisters on earth.

God

Greetings! I hope you find this letter interesting. I want to share information about how God's name is used in the Old and New Testaments. Here are examples of phrases people use when speaking of God:

1) Our Savior
2) Heavenly Father or Father God
3) YHWH
4) Lord God
5) Spirit of the Lord or Spirit of God
6) The Scepter (Genesis 49:10)
7) Elohim, "God, his power and might" (Genesis 1:1, Psalm19:1)
8) El-Elyon, "The highest God" (Genesis 14:17–20, Isaiah14:13–14)
9) El-Olam, "The everlasting God" (Isaiah 40:28–31)
10) El-Roi, "The strong one who sees" (Genesis 16:13)
11) El-Shaddai, "God almighty" (Genesis 17:1, Psalm 91:1)
12) Adonai, "Lord, the lordship of God" (Malachi 1:6)
13) Jehovah (Yahweh), "The Lord, God's eternal nature" (Genesis 2:4)
14) Jehovah-Jireh, "The Lord will provide" (Genesis 22:13–14)
15) Jehovah-Maccaddeshem, "The Lord your sanctifier" (Exodus 31:13)
16) Jehovah-Nissi, "The Lord our banner" (Exodus 17:15)
17) Jehovah-Raha, "The Lord our healer" (Exodus 15:26)
18) Jehovah-Rohi, "The Lord my shepherd" (Psalm 23:1)
19) Jehovah-Sabbath, "The Lord is Hosts" (Isaiah 6:1–3)

20) Jehovah-Shalom, "The Lord is peace" (Judges 6:24)

21) Jehovah-Shammah, "The Lord is present" (Ezekiel 48:35)

22. Jehovah-Tsidkenu, "The Lord our righteousness" (Jeremiah 23:6, *Nelson's Student Bible Dictionary*, 2005).

Before I close this letter, I want to share some of my favorite quotes. "To fall in love with God is the greatest romance; to seek him is the greatest adventure; to find him is the greatest human achievement" (Saint Augustine of Hippo Quotes).

And according to George Washington, "It is impossible to govern the world without God and the Bible."

Abraham Lincoln said, "I believe the Bible is the best gift God has ever given to man. All the good from the Savior of the world is communicated to us through this book."

Moses, the Chosen Hebrew

Hello, I hope all is well. I want to share a bit about Moses's life so that you have some background information on his history. Moses wrote the first five books in Genesis. Noah is Moses's grandfather who lived to be 950 years old (Genesis 9:28). Our roots came from Noah. There were eighteen generations between Noah and Moses.

Noah's three sons were named Shem, Ham, and Japheth, who had their tribes and languages. They had sons and daughters after the flood (Genesis 10:1). "These are the clans of Noah's sons, according to the lines of their descents, within their nations. From Noah's sons came seventy nations that spread out over the earth after the flood" (Genesis 10:32).

From Shem's family tree came Joktan who had thirteen sons. From his thirteen sons, Nahor was born. Nahor had a son name Terah. Terah was Abraham's father. Abraham's family had thirteen generations, and from that family root came Jacob. Jacob had twelve sons and one daughter, even though the Bible mentioned twelve sons; Benjamin was the last son born. Jacob's sons became the ancestors of the twelve tribes in Israel. "All these are the twelve tribes of Israel" (Genesis 49:28). Seventy came from Jacob's family (Exodus 1:5), who were servants in Egypt. Moses came from this family tree.

God told Abraham in his sleep before Jacob was born, "Know for certain that your descendants will be strangers in a country not their own, and they will be servants and mistreated for four hundred years. But I will punish the nation they serve as servants, and afterward they will come out with great possessions" (Genesis 15:13–14). Abraham's family was the beginning of a nation (Genesis 12:2). God promised Abraham that his descendants will inherit the land of Canaan, which is now Israel. God is referring to Jacob and his offsprings who are Moses's immediate family members. Egypt is in the northeast corner of Africa, and that is where Moses was born. Moses's family spent 430 years in this land (Exodus 12:40).

Moses's father was named Amram, who lived to be 137 (Exodus 6:20). Amram married his aunt, his father's sister named Jochebed (Exodus 6:20). Back in ancient days, people married within their family tribes. Moses had a brother named Aaron, and his family was from the Levi tribe.

In Egypt

The kings in Egypt saw that Moses's people, the Hebrew population, were increasing, and they did not like it. Hebrews were God's chosen people called the Israelites, until they returned from the Babylonian exile in the late sixth century BC. From that time on, they become known as a Jew culture. The word *Hebrew* means the "other side" (crossing the Red Sea). If you want to know more about what happened during the time of the king of the Babylonians who captured God's chosen people, read the book of Jeremiah, chapter 20.

One day, the kings from Egypt said, "Look, the Israelites are becoming a large population" (Exodus 1:9). So they felt that they had to stop the Israelites from having more male children. They wanted to control the male population. The kings said, "The Israelites have become much too numerous for us" (Exodus 1:10). They were concerned, if a war started with their enemies, that the Israelites would join them and fight against the Egyptians and leave their country (Exodus1:9–10). Because the Hebrew population was increasing, the kings ordered the midwives to kill every boy born and allowed the girls to live. Again, they wanted to control the male population. "The kings in Egypt said to the Hebrew midwives, whose names were Shephard and Puah, 'When you help the Hebrew women in childbirth, observe them on the delivery stool. If it is a boy, kill him; but if it is a girl, let her live'" (Exodus 1:15–16).

When Moses was born, his mother hid him for three months. She knew she had to do something because Moses was growing big. So "she got a papyrus basket for him and coated it with tar. Then she placed the child in it and put it among the reeds along the bank of the Nile" (Exodus 2:3). The Pharaoh's daughter found Moses. "When the king's daughter opened the basket, she saw the baby and felt sorry for him because he was crying. She said, 'This must be one of the Hebrew babies'" (Exodus 2:6). Moses' sister asked the king's daughter, "Do you want me to get a Hebrew woman to take care of the baby for you?"

She said, "Yes."

And the girl brought the baby's mother (Moses's mother) to care for him (Exodus 2:7–8). Moses's biological mother took care of Moses in the palace, and when Moses "was old enough, she took him to the king's daughter, who adopted him. She named him Moses because she said, 'I pulled him out of the water'" (Exodus 2:10).

Moses lived to be 120 years old (Deuteronomy 34:7). He was raised and educated in the palace with Egyptian kids (Acts 7:22). As he grew older, he realized he was different from the other children. The Egyptian children teased him because he looked and spoke differently. Moses was a foster child. He stuttered and had a speech disorder. Moses grew up angry because he was different from the Egyptian kids and the rest of the family. He ended up killing an Egyptian man and ran away from home.

He spent forty years in Egypt and another forty years in the desert of Midian as a shepherd (Exodus 2:15, Acts 7:30), and his final forty years were spent wandering in the Sinai wilderness with the children of Israel (Deuteronomy 8:2), leading them out of Egypt to the promised land. He wrote the first five books of the Old Testament after leading the people out of Egypt. Little did Moses know God had a big plan for him, just like he has plans for all believers! You can read more about his story in the book of Exodus. Until next time.

Love, Grandma

First Chapter Letter

How God Designed the World

Greetings, grandkids. I hope you are doing well. I am so excited to share with you the first chapter in Genesis. Genesis means beginning. I have faith you will find this letter interesting and that you will learn from it. In Genesis, chapter 1, I will write about how God created the heavens and earth.

God is the *love*. He is the Creator of all things. God is omnipotent, which means all powerful. He is our father, mother, best friend, partner, warrior, and most of all, our leader. God forgives and loves us unconditionally. He loved us before he created us.

God gave his only Son to die on the cross for our sins! "For God so loved the world, that he gave his only begotten son, that whosoever believeth in him should not perish, and have everlasting life" (John 3:16). God chose us to be part of his world! Because of that, we are to love him with all our hearts, love our neighbors, and then ourselves last. Always remember God is in control. It is my opinion that if negative things happened, it is because God has allowed it. It could be because we are paying for our sins or karma. If positive things happen in our lives, it is because God has blessed us. God allows things to happen in our lives to learn from our mistakes and not repeat them.

Jesus's brother James, said we are to rejoice when we are facing trouble times in our life. "Count it all joy, my brothers, when you meet trials of various kinds" (James 1:2) because there will always be a positive end.

In the beginning, God created the heavens, earth, man, and woman in six days. The seventh day was for rest. God created the universe outside of time and space, which means he figured out how he would make everything beforehand. God did not create hell. There is no hell underneath or on top of this world.

Hell, in my opinion, is created by people; hell is karma, our payback from doing sinful things in life. Many people suffer from all sources of problems, but I believe people make their hell.

The book of Genesis is in the Old Testament. It is the first book written in the Bible. I will be calling these letters chapter letters because they are chapters from the Bible and structured on each page differently, like letters to my grandkids. When you read these letters, you should have your Bible next to you to refer to the Bible verses.

God created the earth two thousand years ago. He planted the garden of Eden in the Middle East, known today as Iraq and Syria (*Then and Now Bible Maps Insert*, 2008). They were people of color in that part of the world, Black and Brown. They were labeled the poorest and worst behaved in ancient days, and because of that, I believe God adopted them and called them his people, the Israelites.

Although God chose to adopt the people from the Middle East, he loves us all the same. The color of our skin does not matter. It is what is in our hearts. We are all the same, simply different skin colors. The Bible does not say anything about skin color. However, it does mention other languages. In Genesis 11:7–8, the people in the world spoke one language. God scattered them all over the world because at one point, they were trying to build a city without his approval, the tower of Babel. And because of that, God confused the people with different languages.

God chose the nation of Israel to be his very own people. I believe God chose the Middle East to create the world because he planned on our Lord Jesus Christ to be born in Bethlehem, in the Holy Land, Jerusalem. He also planned on giving the Holy Land to Abraham and his descendants before they were born (Genesis 12:1–3). Jesus was from Abraham's descendants (Matthew 1:1). God had it all figured out beforehand, just like he has our lives planned out if we believe in him!

In Deuteronomy 7:6–7, Moses said, "Israel, you are the chosen people of the Lord God. There are many nations on this earth, but he chose only Israel to be his own. You were the weakest of all the nations."

He chooses the worst people to serve him as he did with me. I was an angry child, teenager, and young adult because my parents, Oscar and Josie Galvez, divorced. I was forced to raise myself for most of my teenage years. I dropped out of high school and had my first son at sixteen years old and two more before twenty-one. I was a single parent for many years and, eventually, went back to school and earned an AA, BA, MA, and doctorate. I went from an angry high school dropout to a successful business owner of twenty years and an author, with God holding my hand one step at a time. God did this for me, and I know he will do it for you if you believe and trust him.

God's Creation

In Genesis 1:1–2, Moses described how God created heaven and earth. And how "the earth was empty, and darkness was everywhere without form, and the *spirit of God* was covering the earth" (Genesis 1:1–2, Isaiah 40:13–14, John 1:3, Acts 17:24). In terms of "empty and darkness without form," it is sharing how there will be times in our life when we will feel empty and in a dark place without direction, but you must trust and believe God can take you out of that dark feeling. "God had a plan when he created the world." He saw the empty and dark space and wanted to bring the light to his world, and he did! Light is used to describe God's Spirit and love that lives in a person. Many people who live a life with love are shining with the light. "If your eyes are bad, your whole body will be full of darkness" (Matthew 6:23). When Jesus spoke to the people, he said, "I am the light of the world. Whoever follows me will never walk in darkness but will have the light of life" (John 8:12).

I was once full of anger and walked in darkness for most of my teenage years and young adult life. I carried that anger with me for

25

many years. My anger hurt a lot of my relationships growing up. I did not have a close relationship with my siblings and parents. I walked around mad all the time until I was introduced to God and his word.

I was in my early twenties when I surrendered my life to God. I asked God to forgive me for my sins, and he did! I have been walking with God for thirty-five years. I know I have his light shining on me. Thank you, Jesus for saving my life! If you feel you are walking in darkness, ask God to forgive you for your sins and ask Him to cleanse your heart and mind so that you can walk in the light. It will help you stay out of trouble. Ask God to come into your life and tell him you believe that his Son died on the cross for your sins and to forgive you for your sins. Once you say these words, God's Spirit will ignite in your body, and you will be a different person. God's Spirit will live in you and help you make the right decisions in life (Galatians 5:16–19). Trust Grandma when I say this!

In terms of *God's spirit* covering the earth, he introduces his Son, Jesus Christ, as his Spirit. "In the beginning was the Word, and the Word was with God, and He was with God at the beginning" (John 1:1 KJSB, 1988; NIV, 1990). The Holy Spirit, Jesus Christ, and God are one, and they were together in the beginning when designing the world and creating humans. His love was covering the earth.

On day one, God created light and darkness and called it day and night (Genesis 1:3–5, Hebrews 11:3, Psalm 74:16).

On day two, God stretched the earth and waters and called it sky (Genesis 1:6–8, Proverbs 8:29, Jeremiah 5:22, 2 Peter 3:5).

On day three, God created the waters to be separated from the land and called the water sea and land ground (Genesis 1:9–13, Psalm 95:5, Hebrews 6:7, Luke 6:4).

God created the stars and moons on day four and marked the seasons, days, years, evenings, and mornings. Thus, the light and day were expended (Genesis 1:14–19, Deuteronomy 4:19).

On day five, God created the birds and the living things in the sea.

On day six, God created the wild animals, livestock, man, and woman in his image, and God told the man to rule over the animals (Genesis 1:20–23; Matthew 19:4; Psalm 104:24, 119:68).

You may ask yourself who God is. How did he create everything? The Bible does not say. What I do believe is that we have a purpose on this earth! We are to believe that our God gave up his only Son to die on the cross for our sins, and we must love our neighbors as ourselves while we are on this earth.

It is getting late, grandkids, until the next time.

Love,
Grandma

Second Chapter Letter

God Finished His Work

Hello, my precious grandkids. I hope all is well, and you are staying in prayer. In this letter, I will share what is written in Genesis, chapter 2. In this chapter, God finished creating the world on the seventh day, and he made the seventh day for resting and called it holy (Genesis 2:1–3, Deuteronomy 4:19, Hebrews 4:4, Isaiah 58:13). All the things that God made were generations of the heavens and earth (Genesis 2:4, Psalm 90:1–2). I believe we are blessed to be participants in God's world and have family, friends, food, music, and each other!

The Garden of Eden

Moses described no rain came from heaven, yet water surfaced the earth, and streams came from the ground (Genesis 2:5). There were no plants and shrubs on the land. But the streams came up from the ground and watered the earth (Genesis 2:6). God was preparing a garden to be cared for by Adam. But first, "God formed the man from the dust of the ground by blowing breath into his nostrils the breath of life, and the man became a living being" (Genesis 2:7, Genesis 7:22).

God planted the garden of Eden in the east part of the world near Egypt, Assyria, Africa, and Babylon. He created the first man's name, Adam, who became the first gardener in the Bible (Genesis

2:8, Isaiah 51:3). Adam's job was to work and care for the garden. In the garden of Eden, all kinds of trees grew from the ground. There were beautiful trees that had colorful leaves and fruits. Trees grew fruits that humans could eat.

God planted unique trees in the middle of the garden that he called the tree of life and the tree of knowledge of good and evil. God told Adam that he could eat from any tree except from the unique trees (Genesis 2:7–9, Revelation 22:2). In the book of Revelation, chapter 2 verse 7, God said, "He who has an ear, let him hear what the Spirit says to the churches. To him who overcomes, I will give the right to eat from the tree of life which is in the paradise with God." People who overcome sin and try to live in love and obedience with God will eat from the tree of life.

In the passage of the tree of knowledge of good and evil, we can see how God lets us know that we will have to choose in life to either live a life of love for others or fall into sinful ways. It is our choice. God instructed Adam not to eat from the Tree of Life. He had a variety of other trees to eat from. God told him, "But you must not eat from the tree of the knowledge of good and evil, for when you eat of it, you will surely die" (Genesis 2:17). God was not talking about killing Adam physically for eating from the tree. He meant the Holy Spirit would die inside of him if he ate from the tree of knowledge of good and evil. When Adam and Eve were made, they were born with the Holy Spirit living in them, and when they ate from the tree, God told them to stay away. The Holy Spirit that lived inside of them died.

When you were born, you have the Holy Spirit living in you. It is not ignited. I believe we are born with the Holy Spirit in us but not activated. We must give our lives to our Lord Jesus Christ if we want the Holy Spirit to start working in your hearts and mind. You can do this by asking God to forgive you for your sins and let him know you believe that he gave his only begotten Son to die on the cross for your sins. Once you have prayed to God, the Holy Spirit will be activated in your heart, and you will be a different person!

After God created the garden of Eden, he made four rivers, one to water the garden of Eden (Genesis 2:10, Psalm 46:4). "A river watering the garden from Eden; from there it was separated into four headwaters." The first river was called Pishon. "It winds through the entire land of Haviah, where there are gold and onyx." Today, the land is known as Saudi Arabia, and the river is called the Rea Sea near Egypt's border. The second river is called the Gihon, which is the Nile River. "It winds through the entire land of Cush," which is Ethiopia today. The third river is called the Tigris. "It runs along the east side of Asshur," which is Assyria today. The fourth river is called the Euphrates. This river runs on the east side of Turkey, Syria, Saudi Arabia, Kuwait, Jordan, and Iraq (Genesis 2:11–14). Finally, the Tigris and the Euphrates meet and run into the Persian Gulf or Arabian Gulf (*Then and Now Bible Maps Insert*, 2018).

God continued to make beasts, birds, and livestock of the fields, bringing them to Adam to name them (Genesis 2:19–20). God gave Adam responsibilities, just like our parents give us chores. God saw that Adam was alone and made a woman for him. Therefore, the "Lord God caused the man to fall asleep; and while he was sleeping, he took one of the man's ribs and closed up the wound with flesh" (Genesis 2:21, Samuel 26:12). "Then the Lord God made a woman from the rib he had taken out of the man [Adam], and he brought her to the man" (Genesis 2:22).

Adam said, "This is my bone of my bones and flesh of my flesh; she shall be called Woman, for she was taken out of man" (Genesis 2:23, Ephesians 5:30, 1 Corinthians 11:8–9). When a man and a woman get married and leave their parents, they become one flesh. When God made Adam and Eve, they were both naked and had no shame (Genesis 2:24–25, Mark 10:6–8).

In terms of Adam working the garden, we too must work in this world. If you do not work, you will not eat, and it will be difficult for you to survive. Do not depend on anyone to care for you when you become of age to work. Take care of yourself and your family. Wives, take care of your husbands and family. Work hard, and God will bless you. Husbands, work hard and support your wife and family. Get your education and find yourselves a job or become an entrepreneur, your own business, like I did.

When you decide to get married and make vows to one another, make sure you understand that this is a lifelong commitment. Marriage could be challenging for some people. Marriage is not a joke. Divorce is heartbreaking, and many can suffer from the breakup. You are one flesh; your wife or husband becomes your partner to the end. Grandkids, it is getting late. I am going to get ready for bed. Until the next time.

Love,
Grandma

Camel ride

Camel

Third Chapter Letter

Adam and Eve Sin

Dear, grandkids. I hope you are well. The last two letters I wrote you were about chapters 1 and 2 of Genesis. Now I will share my interruption of chapter 3 of Genesis. At the beginning of the Old Testament, when God created and designed the earth in chapters 1 and 2 of Genesis, there is no mention of a serpent or an angel that was a devil. Yet, in chapter 3 of Genesis, the first sentence begins with "now the serpent was more crafty than any of the wild animals the Lord God had made" (Genesis 3:1, 1 Chronicles 21:1). The definition of a serpent is a liar, troublemaker, cheat, and snake. "He chained the dragon for a thousand years. It is the old snake, who is also known as the devil and Satan" (Revelation 20:2).

Moses introduces the devil and sin in this chapter. In my studies, I found out that the serpent was once a beautiful angel living in heaven. He was tossed out of heaven along with a third of the other angels who were following him. "And there was war in heaven." Michael and his angels fought against the dragon, and the dragon and his angels fought back. But he was not strong enough, and they lost their place in heaven. The dragon, an ancient serpent called the devil or Satan, leads the whole world astray. "He was hurled to the earth, and his angels with him" (Revelation 12:7–9). The serpent was in heaven fighting the good angels, trying to take over, but God was not allowing that to happen and had the good angels kick the evil angels out (Revelation 12:10–12).

Grandkids, one-third of the angels followed the devil and landed on this earth. The devil convinced other angels to follow him. We are living in a world with evil-spirited people that look beautiful and speak well. These evil people who look like they are your friends will turn on you or influence you to do bad things. Many people are hurt, lonely, and struggling with sin. They want company. I cannot stress enough the importance of having a close relationship with God. The closer you are with the Holy Spirit, the devil will not touch you. It is called spiritual warfare. You will always experience this on earth because the devil is real and wants you to live in sin and be his servant.

The Devil Is Alive

In chapter 3 of Genesis, God instantly tells us that the devil is living on this earth. He is recruiting people to live in sin. We will meet people or know evil and mean-spirited people who work for the devil. The devil comes in many colors and sizes. The devil could look and act like an angel to get what he or she wants from you. Be careful who you associate yourselves with; the devil is a person who manipulates, lies, and will trick you into doing bad things to hurt yourself and others. The devil can be people we know and who are in your circle of friends, families, or neighbors. Moses said the devil is on "earth to lead the whole world astray!" Moses shares an example of how the devil works in Genesis 3:1: "Did God say you must not eat from any tree in the garden?" The devil manipulated Eve to disobey God's instruction. She decided not to listen to God. God told her "not to eat or touch the tree in the middle of the garden" (Genesis 3:2–3, Revelation 22:14). A situation like this you will always face throughout your life. God gives us free will to choose, either to know him personally, live in love for people or sin, and deal with the consequences that come along with it.

In Eve's case, she was weak and listened to the serpent. She looked at the beautiful fruit on the tree and was debating in her mind what to do. "The woman said to the serpent, 'We may eat the fruit from the trees in the garden, but God did say, "You may not eat fruit from the tree that is in the middle of the garden, and you must not touch it, or you will die"""" (Genesis 3:30). The serpent tells Eve, "You will not die" (Genesis 3:4, 2 Corinthians 11:3). God does not want you to eat from that tree because your eyes will be opened, and you will know the difference between good and evil and gain knowledge (Genesis 3:5, Isaiah 14:14, Acts 26:18). Isn't this interesting that God chose Eve to eat the fruit and not Adam? I guess this is how God set it up. But Adam and Eve did not die physically, only spiritually because they disobeyed God and ate the fruit.

Nevertheless, Eve decided to pick some fruit from the tree of knowledge of good and evil. She shared it with Adam, and he ate some. Their eyes and souls immediately realized they were both naked, and they knew the difference between bad and good (Genesis 3:6, 1 John 2:16). They disobeyed God and allowed the devil to win! Shortly after eating from the fruit tree, they gathered fig leaves and made clothes to cover their naked bodies (Genesis 3:7). When was the last time you allowed the devil to win?

The Conviction of Sin

Making clothes to cover themselves was an act of conviction. The definition of *conviction* is "a person guilty of a crime" (*The American Heritage Dictionary*, 2000). This Bible verse is the first time it describes people trying to cover up their sin. I have heard a scholar say it was an act of religion. My interpretation of Adam and Eve's covering up their bodies is that it was a sign of guilt, shame, embarrassment, and they were mad at themselves for not listening to God. So they made themselves clothes to cover up and hide their bodies. They can see evil and good now. They knew they were guilty of sin when they ate the fruit from the tree God told them not to. When you disobey your parents, grandparents, teachers, or anyone loving and caring for you, admit you are wrong. Do not try to cover up your sins and let the devil win because God sees everything bad and good. Come clean before you are convicted and judged.

The Holy Spirit

Let us go back and talk about the Spirit. When God created the earth, "and the spirit of God was covering the waters of the earth," it means several things. First, God our Father, his Son, and the Holy Spirit were present. So "in the beginning, was the Word, and the Word was with God, and the Word was God. He was with God at the beginning" (John 1:1–2). Secondly, when Adam and Eve were born, the Holy Spirit lived in them, but since they ate the fruit and disobeyed God, the Holy Spirit died. That same Holy Spirit that God spoke of when he made the heavens and earth died in Adam and Eve. So when you and I are born, we are born with the Holy Spirit not activated. Our Holy Spirit needs to be started by giving our life to Jesus, as mentioned before.

We all are suffering today because of what Adam and Eve did. We must be reborn if we want the Holy Spirit to be activated. Grandkids, you can be reborn through our Lord Jesus Christ. Reborn means to surrender your life to God. I submitted my life to God when I was living in darkness. I asked God to come into my life and changed my heart. You can surrender your life to God by saying "God, please forgive me for my sins. Cleanse my heart and mind. I believe your Son, Jesus Christ, died and shed his blood on the cross for my sins. I ask this in Jesus's name." Congratulations! If you gave your life to the Lord, this is the beginning of your new life. The Holy Spirit has been activated in your heart! Continue reading these letters because God will speak to you and lead you on the right path!

"The Holy Spirit will teach you everything and will remind you of what I said while I was with you" (John 14:26). The Holy Spirit will come and show the people of this world the truth about sin and God's justice and the judgment (John 16:9). The Holy Spirit will convict you and bring you to repent (Act 17:30). The convicting power of the Holy Spirit opens our eyes to our sin and opens our hearts to receive his grace (Ephesians 2:8, Galatians 5:16).

Consequences for Disobeying God

Let us return to the garden of Eden with Adam and Eve after Adam and Eve ate the fruit. God was walking through the garden, and Adam and Eve heard him, and they ran to hid behind a tree in the garden. God called out to Adam, "Where are you."

Adam said, "I heard you walking in the garden, and I was afraid because I was naked, so I hid."

God said to Adam, "Who told you that you were naked? Did you eat from the tree that I commanded you not to eat from" (Genesis 3:9–11, 1 John 2:28, Ezekiel 18:4, Romans 5:12)?

Adam said, "The woman you created for me gave me some fruit off the tree, and I ate it" (Genesis 3:12, Proverbs 28:13, Luke 14:18).

Adam immediately refused to take the blame for his mistake and confess his sin. He blamed his partner. You will experience this type of situation in your relationships with people. They will not take responsibility for their actions and blame you. Or if you do something wrong, admit to it immediately. Do not try to cover up sin because it will come back and bite you. You will know and see people who will not take responsibility for their wrongdoings. It may be the one you trust the most. All you can do is pray for that person and ask for forgiveness if you are the wrongdoer. And do not get mad and be angry. Do not carry that anger; ask God to help you forgive them. Forgive people and keep going. God said, "I tell you not to try to get even with a person" (Matthew 5:39).

God said to Eve, "What have you done!"

Eve said, "The serpent deceived me and I ate it" (Genesis 3:13, 1 Timothy 2:14, 2 Corinthians 11:3). She made a big mistake! The devil tricked her. Remember that the devil is everywhere on this earth. When you walk outside the door, the devil is sitting and waiting to follow you so that he can trap you into doing sinful things. Suppose you are not sure about something. Pray and ask God to give you direction and guidance. Listen to your gut feelings. Your gut feeling is the Holy Spirit tugging on you to do the right thing. You are always in control of your decisions. Think before you react. "Therefore, put on the full armor of God so that when the day of evil comes, you may be able to stand your ground" (Ephesians 9:13). Jesus told his disciples, "I chose all twelve of you, but one of you is a demon" (John 6:70)!

Jesus's good friend who walked with him for three years turned on him for forty coins. His name was Judas Iscariot. He witnessed Jesus perform many miracles, and he still was unfaithful and did not believe in our Lord Jesus Christ. He betrayed Jesus. God is warning us that we will be betrayed by people who are close to us. If we walk by faith, God gives us grace and love in our hearts for people. In Judas's situation, I believe God's plan for him was to betray Jesus. I feel bad for Judas because he was chosen to play that role in his life. The reason why I say this is because God is in control of everything. If Judas had not betrayed Jesus, he could not have been crucified for our sins. So this act was defiantly in God's plan for us to be saved through his Son, Jesus Christ. I honestly believe each one of us is born on earth for a purpose, a purpose to do God's will, to share his word and live life with love for one another.

Let us go back to the devil. Because the devil manipulated Eve, God put a curse on him. He also gave Adam and Eve lifetime consequences for disobeying him. God said to the serpent, "Cursed are you above all the livestock and all the wild animals! You will crawl on your belly and you will eat dust all day of your life" (Genesis 3:14, Isaiah 65:25, Deuteronomy 28:15–20). Those curses are consequences that affect all of us! Humans are suffering every day because of what Adam and Eve did. People are troubled with depression, illnesses, early death, and diseases that doctors cannot figure out or cure (Leviticus 26:14–26, Deuteronomy 28:15–68). Many of these consequences are passed down to generations because people live in sin and cannot fight against the desires of the world—our flesh. We will always be in spiritual warfare. The spirit and the things on this earth are called the flesh. What I mean by our flesh is we always want what looks and feels good, just like Eve experienced. She saw the fruit, and it was colorful and yummy to the eyes, and she liked the idea of gaining knowledge. We will be in situations like her. For example, I bought seven cars and drove anyone I wanted throughout the week for many years. That was sinful! All I needed was one car to get me around. I could have used the extra money in other ways, maybe pay off my home and rental properties.

Galatians 5:16–17 tells us that if the Spirit guides you, you will not obey your selfish desires. The Spirit and the cravings of our desires are enemies of each other. They are constantly fighting each other and keeping you from doing what is right. The devil and God's angels are in a battle on this earth.

Although I give my tithe every month to my church and have a close relationship with God, my flesh is constantly in battle with material things on earth, and many times it is a waste of money. Some people use their money for sex, drugs, prostitution, gambling, adultery, and alcohol. The list can go on. But my point is we are in God's world. We are to love our neighbors and walk in love with people. It is easy to get caught up in worldly things, material things that can distract us away from God's word. Anything that gets in your way with having a relationship with God is your idol, your God. Examine yourselves. Who and what is most important to you? What is keeping you away from having a close relationship with God?

God told the serpent there would be a time when God will send his Son, made from a woman, and made under the law (Galatians 4:4). And there will be "hostility between you and the woman, and between your offspring and her offspring. He will strike your head, and you will strike his heel" (Genesis 3:15, Galatians 4:4, Matthew 13:25, John 8:44). It is noticeably clear what Moses is saying in this passage. There will be anger and hatred between the devil's family and the woman's family [believers and nonbelievers]. The devil's kids [his offspring/seed] will hate and battle with the woman's kids [her offspring/seed]. There will always be conflict among families. God was prophesying that his Son, Jesus, will come and "strike your head" [the devil], and the devil will strike Jesus's "heel" [bruising on the cross] while on earth (Mathew 1:20–21). But the "God of peace will crush Satan under your feet. The grace of our Lord Jesus will be with you" (Romans 16:20). Jesus eventually wins the battle with the devil! Families and friends, we must believe in our Lord Jesus Christ and get along and have peace with one another, or the devil will win!

God said he would be with us (Romans 16:33 and Micah 5:4–5)! We must trust and have faith!

God cursed Eve because she allowed the devil to trick her. Because of that, God said, "I will greatly increase your pains in child-bearing; with pain, you will give birth to children. Your desire will be for your husband, and he will rule over you" (Genesis 3:16, 1 Timothy 2:12, John 16:21, 1 Corinthians 11:3). This verse says women will be in pain when delivering a baby. The statement describes the pain women will experience with their children in many ways, and women will depend upon their husbands. When a child disobeys their parent, it is very frustrating. It brings hurt and pain to parents because the child refuses to listen. When Jesus's mother, Mary, witnessed her son getting crucified, it hurt her heart and soul. A mother's pain for her child is horrible.

The devil loves to destroy families, friendships, and relationships between marriages, parents, and siblings. Families are constantly in conflict with each other, and they let the devil win! "Everyone will tremble with pain like a woman giving birth: they will stare at each other with horror on their faces" (Isaiah 13:8). "If you had done the right thing, you would be smiling. But you did the wrong thing, and now sin is waiting to attack you like a lion. Sin wants to destroy you, but don't let it!" (Genesis 4:7).

The devil is real on this earth. He even tried to tempt Jesus, but he was not successful. In Luke 4:6, the devil said, "'I will give you all their authority and splendor, for it has been given to me, and I can give it to anyone I want to. So, if you worship me, it will all be yours." Jesus answered and said, "It is written, worship the Lord your God and serve him only" (Luke 4:8).

In Adam's case, because he listened to Eve and disobeyed God by eating the fruit from the tree of good and evil, "the ground will be under a curse," the same ground from where God created men. In other words, God said men would struggle with "painful toil" (Genesis 3:17, 1 Samuel 15:23, 1 Samuel 15:23), hard work, and sweat when trying to grow food. You will see "thorns and thistles" (Genesis 3:18) coming up from the ground, and to the ground you will return. As I mentioned earlier, people are in battle with each other because of sin. And the only way to survive on this earth is by having a relationship with our Lord Jesus Christ. Men will work hard and struggle to raise their families and teach them the word of God. God said they would see "thorns and thistles" coming up from the grounds due to bad seeds (Genesis 3:18). Adam and Eve were bad seeds. Below is an allegory that describes a person planting seeds (God's word).

> A farmer went to sow his seed. As he was scattering the seed, some fell along the path, and the birds came and ate it up. Some fell on rocky places, where it did not have much soil. It sprang up quickly because the soil was shallow. But when the sun came up, the plants were scorched, and they withered because they had no root. Other seeds fell among thorns, which grew up and choked the plants. Still, other seeds fell on good soil, producing a crop—a hundred, sixty, or thirty times what was sown. So he who has ears, let him hear. (Matthew 13:2–9)

Let us go back to the garden where God saw Adam and Eve wearing an outfit made from fig leaves. God did not like they made outfits for themselves. He knew they were trying to be slick. He eventually made Adam and Eve's clothes from "garment of skin" (Genesis 3:21). I think God might have killed an animal for their clothes; if so, this was the first sign of shedding blood from an animal. God covering them with fig leaves is an interpretation of God's love for us, for human life. This passage is connected to Jesus Christ on the cross. Jesus shed blood for our sins. God covered our sins through his Son.

Because Adam and Eve ate the fruit and immediately recognized the difference between good and evil, God made them move out of the garden of Eden. God did not want them to touch any of the fruits in that garden, especially the tree of life that would have allowed Adam to live forever (Genesis 3: 22, Revelation 22:14). God placed an angel called the cherubim who carries a flashing sword to guard the tree of life (Genesis 3:24, Psalm 104:4, Hebrews 1:7) after Adam and Eve were kicked out of the garden of Eden. Angels are real. They live on this earth. In Hebrews 13:2, it says, "Do not forget to entertain strangers, for by doing some people have entertained angels without knowing it."

Adam and Eve thought they could hide and get away with disobeying God. The truth came out. Do not ever try to lie and be dishonest because the truth will always come to light. Whatever you are trying to hide, it will always come to light (Matthew 10:27). It can be a secret you may be holding on to that you told a friend; it will come out. Do not ever think you are not being watched. Remember, God is in control and sees everything you are doing and thinking, bad or good. I am getting ready for bed. Until next time.

Love, Grandma

Fourth Chapter Letter

Adam and Eve's Sons

Greetings, grandkids. I hope you are doing well and treating people with love and respect. In this letter, I will share with you what happened in Genesis, chapter 4. It is the story of Adam and Eve's oldest son, Cain, and youngest son, Abel. When the two brothers were old enough to work, Abel worked and cared for sheep, and Cain was responsible for caring for the grounds, a farmer like his father, Adam (Genesis 4:2, Luke 11:50–51). One day, Cain gave God some of his fruits from his harvest, but it was not the best fruit (Genesis 4:3, Numbers 18:12). Remember in the last chapter's letter, God cursed the ground. "The ground will be under a curse" because of the devil manipulating Eve to eat the fruit. In my opinion, Cain was doomed. The ground was cursed, so it was not going to produce good fruits. Remember I said everything on this earth is planned and laid out the way God designed it.

Cain's younger brother, Abel, worked and cared for sheep. He killed one of his firstborn lambs from his best sheep and gave it to God (Genesis 4:4, Numbers 18:17, Leviticus 3:16, Hebrews 11:4). In the Bible, when people gave things/money to God, it is called an offering. An offering is called a donation that you can give to a church, an organization, or anyone you feel the need to donate. God was pleased with receiving the best offering from Abel and disappointed with Cain's offering. Nevertheless, God praised Abel for his offering, and when Cain saw that, it made him mad. "Cain was so angry that he could hide his feelings" (Genesis 4:5) because God expressed happiness with Abel's offering and not his.

Cain's Negative Attitude

God told Cain, "What is wrong with you? Why do you have such an angry look on your face?" (Genesis 4:6, Proverbs 15:13). "If you would have done the right thing from the beginning, you would be accepted. But since you refused to be kind, sin was waiting to attach you like a loin." God told Cain that sin wanted to destroy him and that he should not let it take control of him (Genesis 4:7). Cain did not understand what God was trying to say to him. He had a bad attitude. Cain allowed the devil to take over! He did not think about the consequence. Cain chose to give God whatever he wanted without thinking about what God wanted. Cain quickly became upset and jealous of his brother. God saw Cain's anger and told him that sin (devil) was waiting to destroy him. God hoped that Cain would confess that he was wrong and turn his negative attitude to positive and ask for forgiveness, but he did not.

In the previous letter, God told Adam he would curse the ground and make it hard for a man to produce good food, remember? Cain's job was working the dirt, so evil was already lurking at him. Cain was doomed from the beginning because that was his role in his life. Yet God tried allowing him an opportunity to repent, but he did not. God was patient with Cain by reaching out to him and pointing out his anger, but Cain was hotheaded and did not listen. We all have a choice to do the right thing or allow anger to control us. You will experience times in your life when you get so upset, mad, or jealous about something. Learn to self-talk. Talk to yourself. Talk yourself into thinking the right way and always think about the consequences. We all have control over the way things are handled in our lives. Stay in constant communication with God and listen to the Holy Spirit. God will help you stay focused. Sin (devil) will always separate you from God. Please do not let that happen!

Let us go back and talk about offerings or gifts to God. In Moses's time, people were required to give a tenth of their goods to God and

LETTERS TO MY GRANDKIDS

the priest, the Levi tribe (Hebrews 7:5–9). In the New Testament, God does not mention offerings or a set amount of money to give a church. Many churches today refer to the Old Testament when talking about tithing 10 percent. I believe you should give whatever you can and to the poor. I give 10 percent to my church and other ministries. Grandkids, what is essential in terms of offerings is giving from your heart. Help your church if you can. God will put in your heart what to do. "Give, and it will be given to you. Good measure, pressed down, shaken together, running over will be put into your lap. For with the measure you use, it will be measured back to you" (Luke 6:38).

Cain Killed His Brother

Back at the farm, Cain asked his brother, Abel, "Let's go for a walk out in the fields". Cain was holding on to his anger toward his brother, and while they were out in the field, Cain killed him (Genesis 4:8, 1 John 3:12). Shortly after, God asked Cain, "Where is "Abel?"

Cain said, "How should I know? Am I supposed to look after my brother" (Genesis 4:9, John 8:44)?

I cannot even imagine talking to God this way if he was talking to me directly. God knew Cain killed his brother. He told Cain, "Why have you done such a terrible thing?" Since Cain murdered his brother, God punished him. He told Cain, "Because you killed your brother and his blood fell onto the ground, you will never be able to farm land again and produce anything" (Genesis 4:10–11, Hebrews 12:24, Revelation 6:10). God told Cain he would spend his life wandering around.

Cain said, "You're making me leave my home and live far from you. I will have to wander without a home, and anyone can kill me" (Genesis 4:12–14, Psalm 51:11).

God told Cain that he did not have to worry about anyone killing him. God put a mark on Cain, letting people know not to touch Cain, and if they did, they would get punished by God. "If anyone kills Crain, he will suffer vengeance seven times" (Genesis

4:15, Psalm 79:12). God forgave Cain, yet he received consequences. He was forced to leave his family and God's presence. He went to go live in the land called Nod, east of Eden, or the wandering land (Genesis 4:16; Jeremiah 23:39). Because of Cain's sin, God told him he would be separated from his family, a perfect example of a consequence. God told Cain he would have his back by not allowing anyone to hurt him, but he still lost in the end because he would be separated from his parents and God's presence. When you kill someone in today's times, you go to prison and lose your family. Family separation affects the entire family. Our God is forgiving. Thus, you will still reap what you have sowed.

The Earth Started Populating

As time passed, Cain eventually married his sister, and they had kids, and their kids had kids. Cain's first son was named Enoch. Cain was so proud of his son he built a city in his name (Genesis 4:17, Psalm 49:11). Enoch had a son and named him Irad. Irad had a son and named him Mehujael. Mehujael had a son named Lamech. Lamech married two of his relatives, Adah and Zillah.

Lamech and Adah had two sons called Jabal and Jubal. Jabal was the first person to build and live in a tent and raise sheep and goats. His brother Jabal was the first person to develop and play harps and flutes (Genesis 4:19).

Lamech and his second wife, Zillah, had a son and daughter. The son's name was Tubal-Cain, who made tools out of bronze and iron, and his sister was named Naamah (Genesis 4:22). Thus, Lamech was the first person mentioned in the Bible to have two wives. Back in those days, having two or three wives was okay, but not in today's times.

Nevertheless, God blessed Lamech's kids with skills to make things, such as instruments that make sounds and music. God blesses all of us with unique gifts and talents. It is up to you to use the gifts and skills to honor God. God gave me many skills. I worked in the construction field as a painter at the age of eighteen. I became a professional painter by trade, and this was the first skill I learned where I earned money. I painted houses, repaired and remodeled homes, and built things most of my life. The second gift God has blessed me with is working with troubled teenage girls and others who have anger problems. I love listening to people and helping them find solutions to their life problems by introducing them to God's word. And my third gift is writing. I enjoy thinking and writing. I had a difficult time in school because I spoke Spanish my first years in school and never learned English correctly. But I never let that stop me from furthering my education and writing. I thank God for all my skills. What are your skills? And are you using them to please God?

Let me go back and talk about Lamech. One day, he called out to his two wives and asked them to listen to what he had to say. "I have killed a man for wounding me, a young man for injuring me" (Genesis 4:23). Lamech wanted his wives to know that they would get punished ten times more if anyone tried hurting him than if anyone tried killing Cain (Genesis 4:23). But whoever he killed were family members because men married their sisters, aunties, and nieces. It is terrible that family members were talking about killing others like it was normal.

The sad part of this story is that Lamech was a grandson of Cain, and he had murder on his mind. He must have known that his grandfather, Cain, killed his younger brother. This type of situation happens in our world today, with families hurting each other. It is sad. Always make peace with family no matter who is wrong. Be the bigger person.

Learn to forgive and love your family members and neighbors as yourself. Life is too short to be mad and to hate. I remember growing up as a teenager and hearing on the news that a father shot and killed his son. It was a famous singer named Marvin Gaye; his father killed him. It was unbelievable. But God tells us by these stories that there will be times like Cain and Abel taking place in this evil world.

God blessed Adam and Eve with another son before they died. His name was Seth. They said that "God has given us a son to take the place of Abel, who was killed by his brother Cain" (Genesis 4:25). Seth was a humble person and loved God. I am almost sure; Adam and Eve told their son Seth about God because he loved and trusted

God. Seth had a son name Enosh, who also had a close relationship with God. Enosh believed in God and had a strong relationship with him (Genesis 4:26). When your kids start having children, please tell them about our Lord Jesus Christ (Psalm 78:5–8). I did that with your fathers since they were babies. Until next time.

Love,
Grandma

Sylvia's oldest granddaughter

Capharnaum in the middle east. The Holy Land

Fifth Chapter Letter

Roots of Adam to Noah

Hello, how are my grandkids doing? I love you so much! I hope you are enjoying the reading. In this letter, you will learn about the descendants of Adam. In Genesis, chapter 5, God created man and woman to be like himself. God called us human beings and blessed us with life (Genesis 5:1–2, Mark 10:6). Please do not get overwhelmed with all of Adam's kid's and grandkid's names.

Adam was 130 when God blessed him with Seth (Genesis 5:3). Seth was more like Adam. He was unique in God's eyes. Adam continued to have sons and daughters and died at 930 years old (Genesis 5:4–5, Luke 3:36–38, Hebrews 9:27). However, Adams's children continued to have children. As mentioned in the last letter, Seth's first son was Enosh. Seth continued to have more sons and daughters and died at 912 years (Genesis 5:6–8, Hebrews 9:27). The following is the list of family members from Adam to Noah. They all had sons and daughters; however, the names listed below are considered the appointed sons:

1) Seth became Enosh's father. Seth means *appointed*.
2) Enosh was ninety years old when he had Kenan and died at 905. Enosh means *mortal*.
3) Kenan was seventy and had a son named Mahalalel and died at 910. Kenan means *sorrow*.

4) Mahalalel was sixty-five when he had a son named Jared and died at 895. Mahalalel means *blessed God*.

5) Jared was 162 when he had a son name Enoch and died at 962. Jared means *shall come down*.

6) Enoch was sixty-five when he had a son named Methuselah and died at 365. Enoch was special. He loved God so much. Enoch means *teaching*.

7) Methuselah was 187 when he had a son named Lamech and died at 969.

8) Lamech was 182 and had a son named Noah and died at 777.

9) Noah was five hundred when he had three sons named Shem, Ham, and Japheth (Genesis 5:9–32).

Noah's father, Lamech, said he came up with the name Noah "because he will give us comfort, as we struggle hard to make a living on this ground that the Lord had cursed" (Genesis 5:29, Luke 3:36). However, the Lamech mentioned in the last letter is not the same one above, in number 7. Noah's father, Lamech, was a godly man who loved God, and the other Lamech from Cain's generation was evil and talked about killing anyone who tried hurting him.

Look at the italicized letters up above, 1 through 6. Seth's name means *appointed*. Enosh means *mortal*. Kenan means *sorrow*. Mahalalel means *blessed God*. Jared means *shall come down*. Enoch means *teaching*. Now let us put these words together: appointed mortal sorrow blessed God shall come down teaching! Amazing, right! I learned this from a Bible teacher, Dr. Chuck Missler. Until the next time.

Love,
Grandma

The Jordan River in Israel

Sixth Chapter Letter

Preparing for the Flood

Hi, grandkids. I hope you all are doing well. These letters will get more interesting as you read along and learn more about Adam's descendants and the devil who roamed around the earth starting trouble (Job 1:7). In Genesis, chapter 6, Noah is introduced in this letter and instructed by God to build a boat because he was getting ready to flood the earth.

Adam's sons continued to have children. The world was increasing with people, and "the sons of God saw that the daughters of men were beautiful, and they married any of them they chose" (Genesis 6:2, Deuteronomy 7:3–4). The "sons of God" are interpreted in the Bible as godly men of Seth's generation (King James Study Bible, 1988; Genesis 5:6–30), who intermarried with ungodly members from Cain's family (the daughters of men), which was unacceptable. Angels are also considered the sons of God (Job 1:7). But in this passage, it could not be talking about angels because angels were not allowed to get married (Matthew 22:30, Mark 12:25). I believe that the falling angels were devils who convicted the females in Seth's family to marry. God warned believers "not to take their daughters for your sons, for they will turn your sons away from following me to serve other gods, and the Lord's anger will burn against you and will quickly destroy you" (Deuteronomy 7:4).

Our Lord Jesus Christ warns us over and over to be careful who we hang around. I always told your parents that "you are what you

53

associate yourself with." We all have a choice and free will to marry who we want. But it is best to marry a person who believes in God. If you marry an ungodly person, I guarantee you will always have problems in your marriage. Jesus said, "If anyone would come after me, he must deny himself and take up the cross and follow me. For whoever wants to save his life will lose it, but whoever loses his life for me and the gospel will save it" (Mark 8:35–36). A nonbeliever will not take up the cross and follow Jesus.

God was upset that godly women married ungodly men and had children. He said, "My spirit will not contend with man forever, for he is mortal, his days will be 120 years" (Genesis 6:3–4, Galatians 5:16). Moses is saying here in this statement that God decreased human life to 120 years. Remember, many people in those days were living long lives, 700–900 years. Today, in our times, people do not live past 120 years.

Nephilim were giant people who were children from the ungodly sons and godly women. These Nephilim were strong and mighty giants. They were warriors of ancient times (Genesis 6:5). God was so upset that he had created men to turn out evil. The sons of God and the daughters of men did whatever they wanted and ignored God. So the Lord said, "I will wipe this human race I have created from the face of the earth, all of the people, animals, and birds of the sky" (Genesis 6:6–7).

Yet God found favor in Noah (Genesis 6:8, Exodus 33:12, Acts 7:46). Noah and his family were the only ones that had a close relationship with God during this time on earth. Everyone else was tricked by the devil and living in sin. "Noah had three sons, Shem, Ham, and Japheth" (Genesis 6:9, 2 Peter 2:5). God told Noah that he was sad because of all the corruption on his earth and that he would destroy it. He could not believe all the violence and trouble that was happening on earth. "Yes, I will wipe them all out along with the earth" (Genesis 6:11–13, Psalm 14:2, Jeremiah 51:13; 2 Peter 2:4–10).

Since God was so disappointed in the world at this point, he instructed Noah to build a boat from cypress wood and waterproof it inside and out with tar. "Make the boat 450 feet long, 75 feet wide, and 45 feet high. Leave an 18-inch opening below the roof around the boat. Put the door on the side, and build three decks inside the boat, lower, middle and upper" (Genesis 6:14–16, Isaiah 34:9, Joshua 2:15). Could you imagine building a boat that size on your property? Your neighbors would probably think you were crazy. I am sure Noah told his neighbors and friends what God told him to do regarding the boat. They probably thought Noah was out of his mind.

God kept Noah and his family safe because they had a close relationship with him and did not follow evil. God does not like sin on his earth, and he is coming one day to judge evil and good. Be ready and know who God is. God will save you and keep you safe as he did with Noah's family. Trust God with all your hearts. No matter what you maybe be experiencing in life, bad or good, God knows everything and is in control! He will see you through tough times. God said to be happy during troubled times because he is preparing something special for you (Jeremiah 29:11).

Noah and his wife and his sons and their wives were the only eight people God kept safe when the flood took place. He told Noah, "I am going to send a flood that will destroy everything that breathes! Nothing will be left alive. But I promise that you, your wife and sons, and daughters-in-law will be kept safe in the boat" (Genesis 6:17, Peter 3:6, 2 Peter 2:5). God instructed Noah to bring along a male and female of every kind of animal in the boat with him. God also told Noah to bring along enough food for his family and the animals. Noah obeyed God and did everything he was told to do (Genesis 6:22).

There was a man named Enoch who walked with God during that time. They had a close relationship (Genesis 5:21–24). And before the flood, God removed him from the earth to not die (Hebrews 11:5). Recall in the last letter, Enoch means teaching. It is incredible how God set up everything. There is no coincidence in life; everything happens for a reason! Until the next time.

Love,
Grandma

Praying at the Western Wall

Seventh Chapter Letter

The Flood

Good morning, grandkids. I hope you are all doing well. Today is Monday, September 1, 2018. In this letter, I will write about what happened in Genesis, chapter 7, how God told Noah to get ready for the flood on the earth. Noah was a faithful man who gave his life to God, and because of that, God saved Noah and his family (Genesis 7:1, Matthew 11:28, 2 Peter 2:5-9).

God instructed Noah to take "7 pairs of every kind of animal that can be used for sacrifice and one pair of all others" in the boat (Genesis 7:2–3, Leviticus 10:10). I will talk to you more about sacrificing because it is an integral part of the Old Testament linked to the New Testament, describing the shedding of our Lord Jesus Christ's blood.

God loved animals and birds that he wanted them on earth, so he made sure Noah put every "pair of clean and unclean animals, of birds and of all creatures that moved along the ground, male and female" on the boat with him as God commanded (Genesis 7:8, Leviticus 11:47). In terms of unclean animals, God was talking about food that was unacceptable to eat. The clean animals were acceptable to eat. There are animals on earth we are not to eat. The Bible does not explicitly say what those animals are.

God said to Noah that in seven days, "I will send rain that will last for 40 days and night and destroy every living creature I made" (Genesis 7:4). Noah, his wife, and three sons—Sham, Ham,

Japheth—and their wives and all the animals entered the boat the same day (Genesis 7:11–12). God closed the door behind them (Genesis 7:16). The flood took place on the "seventeenth day of the second month of the year," which in the Hebrew calendar means the middle of April to the middle of May. Seven days after entering the boat, the floodwaters began to cover the earth (Genesis 7:5–10). Noah was six hundred years old.

Waters came from under the earth and started gushing out everywhere, covering the world. "The sky opened up like windows, and rain came down for 40 days and night" (Genesis 7:11). The water was so deep that the high mountain was sitting twenty-five feet below the water surface. Nothing was left on earth, no humans or animals. "The Lord destroyed everything that breathed" except for Noah, his family, and the animals (Genesis 7:22–23, 2 Peter 2:5). After 150 days, the water started evaporating from the earth. The boat sat on the mountains of Ararat for seventy-four days before they realized the ground was dry.

People were violent and sinful in those days and refused to believe there was a God. They wanted to do things their way, which led to them dying in the flood. "God did promise us that he would never flood the earth again with water" (Genesis 8:21). So we do not ever have to worry about the earth's flooding anymore. Until the next time.

Love,
Grandma

Sylvia standing near the Western Wall

Eighth Chapter Letter

The Water Evaporates from Earth

Hi, grandkids. I hope all is well. In this letter, I will describe what happened in Genesis, chapter 8. Moses first writes of how God reflected on Noah's family and all the animals in the boat. Then he thought about the sinful people and how he destroyed the earth (Genesis 8:1, Exodus 14:21). He destroyed the world because of wicked people. They refused to repent and live right. But God loves us so much that he promised not to end the earth with water again (Genesis 9:15).

Therefore, "God closed the sky, and the rain stopped" (Genesis: 8:2). Then for 150 days, the water started slowly evaporating from the ground. Then God sent the winds over the earth to help fade the seas. "The water receded steadily from the world" (Genesis 8:2, Job 38:37). "The boat stops on the mountains of Ararat," which is in eastern Turkey. There is a place called Noah's Ark National Park in Turkey that outlines the boat structure.

The boat sat on the mountain "on the 17th day of the 7th month of the year." In the Hebrew calendar, it starts from mid-September to mid-October. The boat sat on a high mountain, resting until the water was all gone. Two months later—in the Hebrew calendar, mid-December to mid-January—Noah was able to see the mountaintops on earth (Genesis 8:3–5).

Noah and his family were happy that the rain had stopped, and the water disappeared from the grounds. Noah opened a window forty days later after sitting in the ark on dry land (Genesis 8:6). He decided to send out a raven to see if the grounds were completely dried out, but it kept flying around near the boat, so Noah let the raven come back into the ship (Genesis 8:7). Shortly after, Noah opened the window and sent out a dove. While Noah was looking out the window, he saw the dove flying around the boat. He realized that the dove had difficulty finding dry land, so Noah stretched out his arm through the window, and the dove flew and sat on his hand. Noah immediately pulled his arm back into the boat. He figured that the water was still high above the grounds, so Noah waited seven more days and sent out the dove again (Genesis 8:8–10).

The dove returned this time in the evening, holding a green leaf from an olive tree (Genesis 8:11). Noah and his family were happy they saw the green leaf. They knew it was getting close to exiting the Ark, but Noah wanted to wait another seven days to let the dove out again. This time around, the dove never returned (Genesis 8:12, Jeremiah 48:28). That first day of that year, the water was almost gone. Noah made an opening from the ark, looked through it, and saw the grounds were nearly dried (Genesis 8:13). By the twenty-seventh day of the second month, the earth was dry (Genesis 8:14). In the Hebrew calendar, the second month is from mid-April to mid-May.

God's Promise for the Earth

One year later, Noah was 601 years old. God instructed him to leave the boat with his family (Genesis 8:15–16) after one year. Noah let all the animals out of the boat. They all went their ways in pairs (Genesis 8:17–18). Noah and his family were happy. After that, Noah built an altar where he could offer sacrifices to God. He sacrificed every clean animal and every clean bird and offered burnt offerings to God (Genesis 8:20, Leviticus 11, Exodus 10:25)). Sacrificing animals, grains, fruits, and sweet-smelling spices are gifts to God. There are different types of offering listed in the Bible. In this case, Noah sacrificed an animal, and the smell of the burnt offering pleased God. God said, "Never again will I curse the ground because of man, even though every feeling of his heart is evil from childhood. And never again will I destroy living creature, as I have done" (Genesis 8:21, Exodus 29:18). Interesting that God said these people were evil since they were children. They must have learned to be evil from their home environment. You are your children's first teacher. Learned behaviors start at home first. Please remember you are modeling for your children, and whatever they learn from you will affect their personality and future.

Grandkids, God loves us and does not like to give his children consequences, but we will pay for our mistakes/sins. But he is letting us know that evil spirits will always be lurking even during childhood. Please stay in prayer and rebuke the devil when you feel like sinning. Moses ends the chapter with God saying, "As long as the earth endures, seedtimes and harvest, cold and heat, summer and winter, day and night will never cease" (Genesis 8:22, Isaiah 54:9).

Noah and his family were very patient and humble with the entire process. Noah was old when God chose him to build the ark and sail away. He and his family were in the boat for one year before they step on dry land. We will never know what God has in store for us. God has a plan for all people who believe in him. Until the next time.

Love,
Grandma

Sylvia The sea of Galilee in Israel

The sea of Galilee in Israel

Ninth Chapter Letter

God Made a Promise to Noah (A New Beginning)

Hello, my grandkids. I hope you all are doing well. In this following letter, I will write about what happened in Genesis, chapter 9. Moses shares how God told Noah and his sons to go out in the world and "be fruitful and increase in numbers and fill the earth" with children and grandchildren so people can live everywhere on earth (Genesis 9:1). Back in those days, Noah's sons had children with their wives, and their children had children with their cousins and maybe brothers and sisters. Remember, they were the only ones on earth after the flood. God felt bad for flooding the world that he made a promise with Noah never to flood the earth again (Genesis 9:11–15).

God told Noah and his sons that all the animals, birds, reptiles, and fishes would be afraid of humans (Genesis 9:2, Hosea 2:18). The creatures will be placed under the humans' control, and people can eat them for food. "But life is in the blood, and you must not eat any meat that still has blood in it" (Genesis 9:3–4, 1 Timothy 4:3–4, Leviticus 17:10, Psalm 8:6–8, 1 Samuel 14:33). Even though this statement was meant for the Israelites, not for us, I do not like eating meat with blood in it. However, it is your choice. God did not like the idea of killing and the shedding of blood, regardless if it is humans or animals. God made man in his image, and we are placed on this earth to love one another. "Whoever sheds the blood of a man, by man shall his blood be shed; for in the image of God has God made man" (Genesis 9:5–7, Matthew 26:52).

God's Covenant with Noah and the Earth

God told Noah, "I establish my covenant with you; never again will all life be cut off by a flood; never again will there be a flood to destroy the earth" (Genesis 9:8–11, Isaiah 54:9, Psalm 145:9, Isaiah 54:9). Grandkids, you do not ever have to worry about the earth flooding. God promised he will not do it again. God said, "I have set a rainbow in the clouds over the earth." It's a reminder of the covenant God made between Noah and all living creatures of every kind on earth (Genesis 9:12–17, Ezekiel 1:28, Revelation 4:3, Deuteronomy 7:9). When I see a rainbow, I smile because I know God is around.

Noah's Sons

Noah's three sons—Japheth, Shem, and Ham—and their wives started having children after the flood. Ham later had a son named Canaan (Genesis 9:18–19). Noah's family, at this point, were on dry land near the mountains of Ararat, located in Turkey. They made tents to live in and started populating the world as God asked them.

Noah was known as a vintner, a person who made wines (Genesis 9:20). One day, Noah planted some grapes in his garden, and when the grapes were ripe, he made some wine and drank it. He drank so much that he passed out in his tent naked (Genesis 9:21, Ephesians 5:18). His youngest son, Ham, walked into his father's tent without permission that afternoon and saw Noah naked, lying on the floor uncovered (Genesis 10:24–25). Ham immediately ran outside to tell his two brothers what he saw. The two brothers, Japheth and Shem, grabbed a blanket and walked into Noah's tent backward and covered their dad. They did not want to see their dad naked (Genesis 9:22–23). When Noah woke up and went outside of his tent, his sons Japheth and Shem told their dad what happened. Noah was upset at his son Ham for being disrespectful by walking in his tent without permission. Noah told Ham, "Cursed be Canaan! He will be the lowest of a servant to his relatives" (Genesis 9:25). Noah prayed and asked God to "bless Shem and make Canaan his servant." Noah prayed and asked God to "give Japheth more land and to let him take over the territory of Shem, and may Canaan be his servant" (Genesis 9:26–27, Ephesians 2:13).

As time passes on, Canaan became the Canaanites who were very corrupt in many of the stories in the Bible.

Noah was extremely disappointed and angry with his son Ham that he passed down the consequences to his grandson Canaan who became the Canaanites. Ham disobeyed his father. He should have knocked or called out for his dad instead of walking in his home environment without permission. Obey your parents and anyone who cares for you. Respecting other people's space or home environment is essential.

Noah lived 350 years after the flood and died at the age of 950 (Genesis 9:28). Chapter letters 10 and 11 will outline the generations of Noah's three sons. Until the next time.

Love,
Grandma

The Western wall

Tenth Chapter Letter

The Descendants of the Sons of Noah (Seventy Nations)

Greetings, my beautiful grandkids. I hope life is treating you well. In this letter, I will share with you what happened in Genesis, chapter 10. This chapter lists the descendants of Noah. Recall in the fifth chapter letter, I listed Adam's descendants to Noah and how God blessed Adam with a son named Seth, Noah's great-grandfather (seven generations back). Seth had seven sons, and Lamech was his youngest son, Noah's father (Genesis 5:28–29).

Noah had three sons—Japheth, Shem, Ham—and many descendants after the flood (Genesis 10:1). The sons had land, tribes, and their languages. They had sons and daughters, but only the sons are mentioned in this chapter of Genesis. There were seventy nations created through Noah's descendants. Our roots began with Noah's three sons (Acts 17:26).

Sons of Japheth

Japheth descendants were called the *Japhethites* tribe/nation. Japheth was Noah's older son. He was loved and respected by his father.

Japheth had seven sons (Genesis 10:2, 1 Chronicles 1:5–7). They all had sons and daughters. They settled north of Asia Minor, east of Europe, and west. They were people from Greece, Scythians (European Russians), Cyprus, Medes, and Thracians. If you are interested in the history of Japheth's descendants, please research to learn more about the people and the land. Japheth is known to be the father of Asian people.

Japheth's seven son's names were Gomer, Magog, Madai, Javan, Tubal, Meshech, and Tiras (Genesis 10:2, 1 Chronicles 1:5–7). Gomer had three sons named Ashkenaz, Riphath, and Togarmah (Genesis 10:3). Javan had four sons named Elishah, Tarshish, Kittim, and Dodamin. The descendants of Kittim and Dodamin were called the maritime people who lived on the north side of the Mediterranean Sea. This population loved living and working near the ocean (Genesis 10:4–5, 1Chronicles 1:5–7). They were the sons of Javan, and Japheth was their grandfather.

Sons of Ham

Ham's descendants were called the *Hamites tribe/nation.* Ham is the youngest son. Ham had four sons named Cush, Mizraim, Put, and Canaan (Genesis 10:6, 1 Chronicle 1:1–10). They all had sons and daughters. They settled in the south, west, and north regions, including Canaan, Ethiopia, and Africa. These people were the Canaanites, Egyptians, Philistines, Hittites, and Amorites (dark skin). Recall the name Canaanite came from Ham's son Canaan. An important note to remember is the nation of the Canaanites ends up being the promised land that God told Moses his people/Israelites would eventually inherit—Israel (Exodus 7:1, 34:11–16).

Cush had five sons named Seba, Havilah, Sabtah, Raamah, and Sabteca. The sons of Raamah had two sons named Sheba and Dedan. And Raamah had two sons named Sheba and Dedan (Genesis 10:7)

Ham's oldest son, Cush, had six sons named Seba, Havilah, Sabtah, Raamah, Sabteca, and Nimrod (Genesis 10: 7–8, 1 Chronicles 1:1–9). Nimrod grew up to be a mighty warrior on earth (Genesis 10:9, 1 Chronicles 1:10, Jeremiah 16:16). Cush was the father of Nimrod, who was a warrior and a mighty hunter on earth. His name means "let us revolt." His strength came from the Lord. It was said that "if you hunt like Nimrod, your strength came from the Lord." Nimrod first ruled in Babylon, Erech, and Accad, all of which were in Babylonia. He went to Assyria and built Nineveh, Rehoboth-Ir, Calah, and Resen, between Nineveh and Calah (Genesis 10:8–12; Micah 5:6).

Mizraim had seven sons name. They are the Luddites, Anamites, Lehabites, Naphtuhites, Pathrusites, Casluhites (from whom the Philistines came from), and Caphtorites (Genesis 10:13–14).

Canaan (Canaanites) had eleven sons and tribes/nations, including his firstborn Sidon and Heth (Genesis 10:15, Jeremiah 47:4), and the Hittite, Jebusite, Amorite, Girgashite, Hivite, Arkite, Sinite, Arvadite, Zemarite, and Hamatite cultures (Genesis 10:16–19, 1 Chronicles 1:15–16). The Canaanites eventually spread from the territory of Sidon and went as far as Gaza in the direction of Gerar. They also went toward Sodom, Gomorrah, Admah, and Zeboiim (Genesis 10:20).

Sons of Shem

Shem's descendants were incredibly special people called the *Semites tribe/nation*. Abraham, David, and Jesus were from Shem's family line. Shem had five sons named Elam, Asshur, Arphaxad, Lud, and Aram, and they all had sons and daughters. They settled in the southern region which included Arabia, Syria, Assyria, and Persia. Shem's son Lud traveled to Lydia, the central West Asia Minor.

Aram had four sons named Uz, Hul, Gether, and Meshech (Genesis 10:23, Job 1:1)

Arphaxad had one son named Shelah, and Shelah had one son named Eber.

Eber had two sons named Peleg and Joktan, and during these days, the earth was already divided (Genesis 10:25, 1 Chronicles 1:19).

Joktan had thirteen sons. Their names are Almodad, Sheleph, Hazarmaveth, Jerah, Hadoram, Uzal, Diklah, Obal, Abimael, Sheba, Ophir, Havilah, and Joktan (Genesis 10:26, 1 Chronicles 1:20–22).

Noah's son Japheth was the oldest; Shem, the second; and Ham, the youngest. They populated worldwide after the flood (Genesis 10:32). However, they were all in the Middle East part of the world, divided. Japheth's family settled the North, West, and East. Ham and Shem, for the most part, stayed in the south region. Their kids spread out to other parts of the west and east. The tragic thing is that they all ended up divided and formed armies, kings, high priests, leaders, and idols to worship. They fought against one another for land, servants, and goods. Yet they were all family members who forgot their roots, which some people are doing today, forgetting their roots.

We are in this world to love our families, friends, and neighbors, just like Jesus did when he walked on this earth. I cannot say this enough because we are all related. Until the next time.

Love,
Grandma

The Dome of the Rock in Jerusalem

Eleventh Chapter Letter

The Tower of Babel

Greetings, grandkids. I hope you are all in good health and taking care of yourselves. I am at work, and today is Thursday, December 9, 2019. I have some free time, so I decided to open my laptop and pick up where I left off. I will be writing about what took place in Genesis 11.

Moses begins by sharing that Noah's sons and their kids were all speaking one language and had to move eastward toward a place called Shinar (Genesis 11:1–2). Shinar was in the region of Babylon, and it is called Iraq today, fifty-nine miles west of Baghdad. They all settled in Shinar and started building themselves a city and a tower, a tower to reach the heavens, at least that is what they thought. According to the Bible, they wanted to make themselves famous. They did not want to move around the world as God asked them. "They said, come let us build ourselves a city, with a tower that reaches the heavens, so that we may make a name for ourselves and not be scattered over the face of the whole earth" (Genesis 11:3–4).

God said, "No, hold up! You guys are not going to build anything without my approval." And because of that, the Spirit of God came down from heaven and said, "You all are speaking the same language and think you can do whatever you want?" (Genesis 11:5–6, Psalm 2:1). God confused their language on purpose so they would not understand one another (Genesis 11:7). They babbled among each other and were confused. They did not understand each other.

They were divided and went on their separate ways (Genesis 11:8, Luke 1:51). Today, there are more than three thousand languages and dialects in the world (The King James Study Bible, 1988).

The Lord scattered all of Noah's descendants around the earth with new languages. They eventually stopped building the city and called it the tower of Babel (Genesis 11:9). God did not like that they were making a city without his approval. God wants us to ask him for direction and help when we want or decide to do something in our lives. There will be many things you may want to do, but get in the habit of praying first and asking God to give you direction. I always have to remind myself before making any plans. I pray beforehand and ask God for guidance. For example, I may spend money on things I want and not what I need. I do try to practice every day to include God in what I am thinking about doing. I find myself saying, "God, if it is your will, please let this or that happen." Stay in constant prayer and ask God to show you what is right, especially if you need help making big decisions.

From Shem to Abraham

The rest of Genesis, chapter 11 verse 10–30, continues to list Shem's family tree. "Two years after the flood, Shem had a son name Arphaxad, at 100 years old" (Genesis 11:10). He lived to be five hundred and had sons and daughters. The following is a list of Shem's descendants (Genesis 11:10–24):

- When Arphaxad was 35, he had Selah and other sons and daughters. He lived 403 years (Genesis 11:12–13).
- When Selah was 30, he had Eber and other sons and daughters. He lived 403 years (Genesis 11:14–15).
- When Eber was 34, he had Peleg and other sons and daughters. He lived 430 years (Genesis 11:16–17).
- When Peleg was 30, he had Reu and other sons and daughters. He lived 209 years (Genesis 11:18–19).

- When Reu was 32, he had Serug and other sons and daughters. He lived 207 years (Genesis 11:20–21).
- When Serug was 30, he had Nahor and other sons and daughters. He lived 200 years (Genesis 11:22–23).
- When Nahor was 29, he had Terah and other sons and daughters. He lived 119 years (Genesis 11:24–25).
- When Terah was 70, he had Abram, Nahor, and Haram. He lived 205 years (Genesis 11:26, Joshua 24:2).

Terah's Family Line

Terah was the father of Abram, who is Abraham. God changed his name (Genesis 17:5). Nahor and Haram are Abraham's brothers (Genesis 11:27).

Haram had a son name Lot and a daughter. Nahor married his niece, Milcah, daughter of his brother, Haram (Genesis 11:29). Back in those days, family members married within their families. Haram eventually died in Ur of the Chaldeans where his family lived. Terah decided to move from that place and went south of Mesopotamia, known today as Iraq. He wanted to take his family to the land of Canaan but settled in an area called Haran, about six hundred miles northwest of Ur (Genesis 11:31, Nehemiah 9:7). But before they moved, his son Abraham married his niece, Sarai (named changed to Sarah, Genesis 17:15–16), who could not have children (Genesis 11:30, Luke 1:36).

Abraham's brother Nahor married Milcah, his niece, and they were their nephew Lot's sisters (Genesis 11:30–31). I know this sounds crazy, uncles marrying their nieces, but this was how the world was populated in those days.

There are fifty chapters in the book of Genesis, and we went over twelve. The first eleven shared stories of events that took place with human beings. The same stories in those chapters are happening in our world today and in our families. There were strong messages in those letters regarding loving your neighbors as yourself and staying clear of sin to avoid consequences/karma.

Chapter 11 shared how God separated families throughout the world and changed their languages and a list of Terah's family tree, Abraham's father.

The following letters will focus on Abraham's family life and how God promised Abraham that he would give his descendants a great nation. In the following fourteen letters, I will talk about Abraham, his wives, and their children's life stories. Moses wrote about Abraham and his family's trials and tribulations, many of the same family problems we are experiencing today. Abraham's life story is shared in Exodus 2:24, Matthew 1:1–2, Luke 3:34, Acts 7:2–8, Romans 4, Galatians 3, and Hebrews 11. He is known to be the forefather of both the Jews and Arabs. Until the next time.

Love,
Grandma

Twelfth Chapter Letter

Abraham Was Chosen

Dear, grandkids. I hope you are following along with your Bible. I am trying to make the book of Genesis easy for you to understand. In chapter 17 verse 4 of Genesis, God changed Abram's name to Abraham, which means "High Father" in Hebrew, and changed his wife's name Sarai to Sarah (Genesis 17:15–16). And because of that, I will use their changed names from this point on to make it easier to follow along.

In the following letters, from Genesis 12 through 25, I will write about Abraham, his wife, Sarah, and their family's trials and tribulations. I will share with you about Abraham's relationship with God and the promises God made to Abraham. I will talk about Abraham and his family's struggle with the flesh, the things of the world, how Abraham struggled with his spirit, and how Sarah asked Abraham to marry her servant so they could have a child.

In this chapter of the Bible, Moses tells how the Lord talked to Abraham when he was seventy-five years old (Genesis 12:4) in a vision. God told Abraham to leave his country, in Ur in ancient Sumeria (Mesopotamia), with his family and relatives, and go to a land where "I will show you" (Genesis 12:1 and Acts 7:2–3). He listened and obeyed God but did not leave right away. Abraham waited five years after his father died and moved. Then he settled in Haran (Acts 7:4) and eventually ended up in Canaan. Abraham is referred to as the Father of the Faithful (Hebrews 11:8), Father of all Nations

(Genesis 17:4), and a friend of God's (James 2:23). His name is mentioned in the New Testament seventy-four times.

God had plans for Abraham and his descendants. He was a chosen man to save and lead the Israelites out of Egypt. Abraham was the founder of the Jewish nation. Our Lord Jesus Christ came from his descendants. God promised Abraham to give him the land of Canaan, which is Israel today, the Holy Land. Little did he know what God had in store for him. Do you ever listen to what God is saying to you? I know it could be challenging to hear and pay attention to him. But through prayer and reading his word, he will listen and talk to you. God is on every page of the Bible.

When Grandma's Life Changed

My spirit was tugging on my heart to return to school to further my education, and when I was twenty-eight, my first real job was a painter. I was eighteen years old when I started working in the construction field as a painter. I loved it, but after ten years of painting all types of buildings, houses, different structures, and climbing up and down ladders throughout San Diego County, I was getting a bit overwhelmed.

I felt that burning desire to return to school to learn how to learn. I prayed and made that move to quit painting and attend college full time. Most of you know that I was a high school dropout with three boys at twenty-one years old. I went back to school and earned my college degree. My point is, God has a plan for all of us. My spirit told me to go back to school. I stepped out in faith and believed God had my back, just like Abraham. We both walked by faith and could not see God holding our hands. We just trusted and believed. You must listen to the spirit that lives inside of you. Believe in your dreams and always pray and walk with God. He will show you the way. He will put people in your life to help you along the way, just as he did with Abraham and me. My spirit encouraged me to write this book, and I know the Holy Spirit is always with me. When I have questions about anything in terms of God's word, the

Holy Spirit leads me to the answer. And the Spirit that lives in you will do the same for you.

Good morning. Today is February 22, 2020. It is 3:00 a.m. I could not sleep, so decided to get up and write to you.

Abraham's Life Journey

God chose Abraham and blessed him tremendously! God knew his heart and soul. God told Abraham, "I will make you into a great nation and I will bless you, your descendants, and I will make your name great, and you will be a blessing; I will bless those who bless you, and whoever curses you I will curse and all people on earth will be blessed through you" (Genesis 12:2–3). I believe God described our Lord Jesus Christ through Abraham's seeds (Matthew 1:1). We too are his seeds.

Abraham obeyed God and took his wife Sarah and nephew Lot with him. They packed up everything they owned and traveled to the land of Canaan (Genesis 12:4–6; Deuteronomy 11:30, 10:18–19). It must have taken them months to travel by foot. It was 600–700 miles from their home in Ur to Canaan. During those days, there were religious wars and the trading of goods and servants. They had to walk through deserts and over hills. They walked through a land called Shechem, where there was a tree known as "the great tree of Moreh" north of Jerusalem, where the Canaanites lived (Genesis 12:6, Hebrews 11:9). Keep in mind, these places were all located in the Middle East part of the world. (For example, these places were in the east, west, north, and south parts of Israel, Jerusalem, Egypt, Assyria, Syria, Judah, Lebanon, Africa, Hurrian, Babylonia, Arabia, Mesopotamia, and the Mediterranean Sea.)

The Lord spoke to Abraham again while traveling through the land of Canaan and promised him that he would give him that land. "I will give this land to your family forever." And because of that, Abraham built an altar for the Lord and worshiped him (Genesis 12:7). After that, he continued to travel toward the east country hills of Bethel and Ai. Abraham made a tent there and stayed awhile with his family. Bethel was facing the west, and Ai was facing east (they were twelve miles north of Jerusalem). Abraham built another altar there for God and worshiped him (Genesis 12:8–9). Abraham loved and trusted God so much that he showed him by building altars to pray and honor him. However, God knew his heart was good.

Abraham packed up again and traveled toward the south desert in Israel. He did not stay in the desert long because the land was dry and challenging to harvest, so he decided to travel to Egypt (Genesis 12:10–11).

On their way to Egypt, Abraham told his wife Sarah, "You are so beautiful, and I would hate for the Egyptians to kill me because I am your husband and take you away from me." And because of that, Abraham asked Sarah to lie to the Egyptian kings. He said, "Sarah, can you please say you are my sister so that they won't kill me" (Genesis 12:12–13).

Abraham knew that the pharaoh officials would lust over his wife. The pharaohs were the rulers and kings over the people in Egypt. Abraham and Sarah are stepsiblings. "They both had the same father but different mothers" (Genesis 12:20).

As Abraham was approaching Egypt, at that moment, he showed fear. He was afraid of the rulers and forgot to put his trust in God at that moment. Even though God had his back the entire time, he failed and lost faith. In life, we will make this same mistake. But we must try and remember God is always with us, and he will protect us. He said, "If you remain in me and my words remain in you, ask whatever you wish, and it will be given to you (John 15:7). Abraham was afraid of getting killed and losing Sarah, so they lied.

When Abraham and his wife arrived in Egypt, the officials saw how beautiful she was and reported it to the king (Genesis 12:14). The king immediately brought Sarah up to the palace and treated her kindly. Abraham was treated with respect and honor because the king wanted Sarah (Genesis 12:15–16). They gave Abraham's sheep, cattle, donkeys, camels, and servants since the king believed he would keep his wife, Sarah, for his wife.

The following days, the king approached Abraham and said, "You made me believe this was your sister, and I have married her. She is your wife, not mine! Why didn't you tell me she was your wife?" Why did you say she was your sister? Take her and go" (Genesis 12:17–19, 1 Chronicles 16:21, Psalm 105:14)! God inflicted a disease on the king and his entire family in the palace because he took Sarah into his home and made her his wife. He blamed Abraham and wanted them off the land. The king told his men to allow Abraham, Sarah, and his nephew Lot to take everything given to them (Genesis 12:20, Proverbs 21:1) and make them leave the land. The king believed in Abraham's God because of the diseases that immediately came upon them. Abraham and Sarah lied instead of trusting God to protect them. Lying is a bad habit that can get you trapped. Be honest!

As mentioned before, God always protected and had Abraham's back. Abraham was the one that lacked faith during that incident. You will be in situations where you forget that God is with you, but you will never forget he is holding your hand if you stay in constant prayer. Until the next time.

Love,
Grandma

Grandkids

Thirteenth Chapter Letter

Abraham and His Nephew Lot Separate

Hello, my grandkids. I hope you are enjoying the letters. In chapter 13 of Genesis, Abraham left Egypt and traveled back to Negev (southern part of Israel) with his wife and Lot (Genesis 13:9). Abraham was very wealthy at this point with livestock, silver, and gold (Genesis 13:1–2). When he arrived in Negev, he traveled to different small towns trying to find a place to settle. He decided to stay in Bethel to build his tent where he previously made the first altar to God (Genesis 13:3–4).

Abraham had shared his wealth with his nephew Lot. He gave Lot some of his flocks, herds, tents, and servants. They were both wealthy. God blessed them abundantly. They had so many goods that it became overwhelming for them. Abraham's and Lot's men began arguing because of limited space (Genesis 13:6). The Canaanite and Perizzite tribes were also living near them (Genesis 13:7).

Because Abraham did not like conflict, he told his Nephew Lot, "Let's not have any quarreling between you and me or between our herdsmen. We are family" (Genesis 13:8). Abraham told Lot they need to separate and go their ways. Abraham wanted peace, so he told Lot to look ahead and see the land in front of them. "Let us part and go our separate ways. If you go to the left, I'll go to the right, or if you go to the right, I'll go to the left" (Genesis 13:9, Romans 12:18).

Abraham allowed Lot to choose where he wanted to live first. Lot looked up and saw how green and beautiful the land looked near the plain of Jordan. It was beautiful, like the garden of Eden. So he decided to settle east of Abraham near Sodom. Abraham lived in Canaan (Genesis 13:10–12, Isaiah 51:3). Lot did not think twice about moving to the plain of Jordan. He focused on how beautiful the land looked and did not think about his environment. Lot and his men pitched their tents, made themselves comfortable in their new community. They moved nearby a city called Sodom and Gomorrah. "The men of Sodom were wicked and sinning against the Lord" (Genesis 13:13–14).

Abraham was a kind and gentle man. He was patient with his nephew Lot. Abraham's character toward his nephew was humbling. He shared his wealth and was not concern about getting more prosperous.

God Promises to Abraham

Shortly after the two separated, the Lord spoke to Abraham and said, "Lift your eyes from where you are and look to the north, south, east, and west. All the land you see I will give to you and your offspring forever. I will make your offspring like the dust of the earth, so that if anyone could count the dust, then your offspring could be counted" (Genesis 13:15–16, Acts 7:5). God told Abraham to "walk through the land, take a deep breath and look at the land I am giving you" (Genesis 13:17, Numbers 13:17–24).

Abraham did not say anything when God was showing him the promised land. He just packed up his men and belongings and moved his tents to live near the oak tree of Mamre at Hebron, south of Jerusalem. Abraham loved and honored God, and he demonstrated it by building altars to worship him. It seemed like Abraham built altars to the Lord every time he felt honored or blessed by him. Abraham built three altars to glorify God. I purchased a building twelve by twenty and called it the Lord's Temple. It is located on the east side of my property. I decorated it inside and out to make it look like paradise, a temple. It is a place for me to have quiet time with the Lord, to study his word, and teach. I held church in the temple and group sessions daily or sometimes weekly with the grandkids. I understand how Abraham felt wanting to give something of value to God. Find a space in your home or build a place where you can dedicate it to God. It will be your special place for you and God! Until the next time.

Love,
Grandma

Grandkids in Temple

The Temple

Fourteenth Chapter Letter

Nine Kings at War and Abraham Rescues Lot

Greetings, my beautiful grandkids. Today is Friday, April 10, 2020. It is Good Friday, which means Jesus died on the cross for our sins on Friday. Easter is in two days. I feel terrible we cannot celebrate Easter, Jesus's resurrection, after he died on the cross for our sins. God loved the world so much he gave his only Son to die on the cross for our sins. That is what Easter is all about! Our world is currently going through a crisis. It is called a coronavirus disease, and it is spreading across the globe. We must isolate ourselves and not gather according to the California government. You guys may remember this situation.

In chapter 14 of Genesis, Moses writes about nine kings. Four of the kings ruled over five kings for twelve years, and in the thirteenth year, the kings rebelled and came together at a place called Siddim Valley to discuss attacking other tribes. The Siddim Valley is now covered by the southern part of the Dead Sea (Genesis 14:1–4, Deuteronomy 29:23, Numbers 34:12).

The nine kings are listed below:

Shemites	versus	Hamites
1) King Amraphel of Babylonia		1) King Bera of Sodom
2) King Arioch of Ellasar		2) King Birsha of Gomorrah
3) King Chedorlaomer of Elam		3) King Shinab of Admah
4) King Tidal of Goiim		4) King Shemeber of Zeboiim
		5) King of Bela, known as the city of Zoar

A War between Nine Kings and Abraham

A year later, King Chedorlaomer of Elam and his allies attached and defeated the Rephaites in Ashteroth-Karnaim, the Zuzites in Ham, and the Emites in Shaven-Kiriathaim. They also beat the Horites in the hill county of Edom as far as El-Paran, near the desert (Genesis 14:5–6, Deuteronomy 2:12). They eventually went back to Enmishpat, known as Kedeah, and conquered the entire territory of the Amalekites and the Amorites who were living in Hazaon Tamar (Genesis 14:7, 2 Chronicles 20:2).

Later, the five kings turned and battled with the four kings while they were in the Valley of Siddim (Genesis 8–9). The city was full of tar, and when the kings and the army men of Sodom and Gomorrah ran, some of the men fall in tar while others ran to the hills (Genesis 14:10). The four kings snatched up all the goods and food that belonged to Sodom and Gomorrah and fled. They also captured Lot, Abraham's nephew, and his possessions (Genesis 14:11–12). An army man witnessed everything and escaped and went to Abraham and reported what took place (Genesis 14:13).

One army man escaped telling Abraham what was going on regarding the war and how they captured his nephew Lot. Recall, Abraham was living near the great oak trees that belonged to Mamre, the Amorite; they were Abraham's allies (Genesis 14:12–13). Abraham was not happy about this situation when he heard about it. He gathered 318 of his trained army men at night and divided them up to attack those four kings and their allies (Genesis 14:14–15, Ecclesiastes 2:7, Isaiah 41:2–3). Thus, Abraham's men won the battle and chased them off to the north of Damascus.

Abraham and his men rescued Lot, his wife, and their possessions (Genesis 14:16). After Abraham returned from defeating King Chedorlaomer and his men (Genesis 14:17, 1 Samuel 18:6), the king of Sodom sent a message to Abraham asking if he could meet him in the King's Valley to talk.

The king of Sodom told Abraham, "All I want is my people; you can have everything else" (Genesis 14:21).

Nevertheless, in terms of Lot, I think he made some bad choices hanging out with unbelievers. They did not believe in God, and they worshiped idols. He should have never got involved with those men who eventually turned on him. There will always be people in your life that will do the same. Do not be surprised. God said there would be days when family and friends will turn against each other, which will hurt you deeply (Matthew 10:36 and Luke 21:16). When you experience this, you must forgive them.

King Melchizedek and Abraham

In chapter 14 verse 18, Moses makes a quick transition and writes about a king named Melchizedek. He was a godly man who loved the Lord our God. I believe he was God's messenger.

King Melchizedek of Salem was not part of the nine kings. Moses shares how King Melchizedek was a priest of God Most High. King Melchizedek gave Abraham some bread and wine and said, "I bless you in the name of God Most High, creator of heaven and earth. All praise belongs to God Most High for helping you defeat your enemies" (Genesis 14:18–20, Acts 16:17, Hebrews 7:4, Ruth 3:10). Abraham was honored and pleased to hear the compliment. In return, he gave him a tenth of everything he had. I think King Melchizedek was sent by God to let Abraham know that God helped him win the battle against the kings' army. God was always present. God said he would never leave us or forsake us (Deuteronomy 31:6).

God will always fight our battles, if we allow him to as he did with Abraham. We must trust and believe God has our back no matter what we are experiencing in life. Always stay in prayer and communicate with our Lord Jesus Christ.

In terms of Abraham giving a tenth of his goods to Melchizedek, it was a message to us. We must give back and share our money and goods. Give to your church and/or help poor people. I used to give clothes to poor people who lived in Tijuana and the Goodwill. Remember, we are in this world to love one another and help each other. But do not let people take advantage of you. Always pray and ask God to help you decide.

Back to Genesis 14:21, the king of Sodom was convincing Abraham to give him back his men. Abraham did not want any of his property. Abraham told the king, "The Lord God Most High made the heaven and the earth, and I have promised him I wouldn't take anything of yours, not even your sandal strap or a piece of thread because I do not want you to tell others, you made me rich" (Genesis 14:22–23, Daniel 12:7, 2 Kings 5:16).

It is clear Abraham prayed before he went into battle against the kings because he told the king of Sodom that "I made a promise to God that I would not take anything from you, not even your sandal strap or a piece of thread." Abraham was not a greedy man. He was a kind man toward his neighbors.

An interesting side note: the kings attacked men who were giants. The giants were the children of Seth who intermarried with Cain's evil descendants who were warriors. They were the Rephaites, Zuzites, and the Emites (the Nephilims). These giants were the devil's kids. Recall back in Genesis 6:4, the Nephilim were on the earth in those days, "when the sons of God went to the daughters of men and had children by them." The sad part of this war story is that these men were all related, stemming from Noah's sons. Until the next letter.

Love,
Grandma

Grandkids

Fifteenth Chapter Letter

God's Promises to Abraham

Hi, grandkids. I hope you are all doing well. Today is Monday, May 6, 2020. I am at work. I had some free time and wanted to get back to writing you. In Genesis, chapter 15, God talked to Abraham and made several promises to him. The Lord said he would take care of him throughout his life and his descendants.

God said, "Do not be afraid, Abraham. I will protect you and reward you greatly" (Genesis 15:1).

Abraham answered, "God, you have given me everything I can ask for, except children. And when I die, my good friend, Eliezer from Damascus, his servants and my servants will inherit everything" (Genesis 15:2–3, Habakkuk 3:1, Acts 7:5).

God said, "No, they would not! You will have a son of your own, and everything you have will be his." God told Abraham to come outside and look up to the sky and see if he could count the stars because that is how many descendants he would have (Genesis 15:4–5, 2 Samuel 7:12). Abraham believed and trusted God (Genesis 15:6, Galatians 3:6, Romans 4:3).

In Genesis 15:7, God reminded Abraham that he brought him out from Ur in Chaldea and gave him the land he was currently living in. Abraham asked God, "How can I know the land will be mine" (Genesis 15:8, Luke1:18)? Here Abraham wanted God to give him validation. I too need proof. I need to know if God is listening to me when I pray. Especially when I study his word and do not understand something, he helps me find the answers.

The Lord told Abraham to "bring him a three-year-old cow and a three-year-old female goat, a three-year-old ram, a dove and a young pigeon" (Genesis 15:9). Back in those days, people killed animals to shed blood so that their sin could be forgiven or, in this case, to make a statement. Abraham obeyed God, cut the animal in half, and laid the two halves of each animal on the ground. However, Abraham did not cut the doves and pigeons in half. The birds in the air tried to eat the cut-up animals, but Abraham chased them away (Genesis 15:10–12).

As it was getting dark, Abraham fell asleep. Then God spoke to him while he was sleeping. First, the Lord told Abraham he would live to be old and die in peace. Second, God promised Abraham that his descendants would live as foreigners in a land that does not belong to them (Egypt). They will be forced to be servants and abused for four hundred years, but it was indeed 430 years (The New King James Study Bible, 1988). Third, God told Abraham the nation who enslaved them would be punished. Finally, God said to him that his descendant would leave the land with many possessions.

Four generations later, Abraham's descendants will return and take the land (Canaan/Israel). The Lord told Abraham that the people living there would be sinners, and they will be punished (Genesis 15:13–16, Acts 7:6–7, Exodus 15:14, Matthew 23:32).

While Abraham was still asleep, it was dark, and a flaming fire of smoke was in the air between the two halved animals. Right at that moment, the Lord made a promise to Abraham. He said, "I will give your descendants the land east of the Shihor River on the border of Egypt as far as the Euphrates River. They will have the land of the Kenites, the Kenizites, the Kadmonites, the Hittites, the Perizzites, the Rephaites, the Amorites, the Canaanites, the Girgashites, and the Jebusites" (Genesis 15:17–21, Exodus 23:31, Joshua 1:4, 2 Kings 7:6).

God promised Abraham that his descendants would make up the nations mentioned above. The flaming fire of smoke in the air was a symbol of God's promise to Abraham. He was serious. Until the next time.

Love,
Grandma

Grandkids

Sixteenth Chapter Letter

The Egyptian Servant
Woman and Her Son

Good morning, grandkids. I hope you are all doing well. I love you. Today is Wednesday, May 20, 2020. I am at home this evening, and I will be writing you about Abraham, Sarah, and her Egyptian servant woman named Hagar who had an intimate relationship with Abraham. With Sarah's approval, Hagar and Abraham married and had a son named Ishmael.

In Genesis 16, Moses writes how Sarah had not been able to have any children (Genesis 16:1). Sarah owned a servant woman named Hagar, and she said to Abraham, "The Lord has not given me any children, can you sleep with my servant, and if she has a child, it will be mine" (Genesis 16:2).

Abraham agreed, and Sarah gave him her servant woman, Hagar, to be his wife. This took place after Abraham and Sarah lived in Canaan for ten years. When Hagar heard the news, she was happy and started oppressing Sarah (Genesis 16:3–4). Sarah did not appreciate Hagar's attitude and blamed Abraham.

"It's all your fault!" Sarah told Abraham. "I gave you my servant, and she has been treating me mean ever since she was pregnant." Sarah blamed Abraham. "You have done me wrong, and you will have to answer to the Lord for this" (Genesis 16:5).

The two women were jealous of each other. But it was Sarah who permitted Abraham to be with Hagar to have a child. It was Sarah's self-desire. She should have waited upon the Lord.

Sarah made a big mistake! Abraham should have disagreed with Sarah. Instead, he listened to her and did what she requested. This situation reminded me of Eve convincing Adam to eat the fruit. Abraham and Sarah lacked faith during this incident. Abraham should have stepped up and said no to Sarah!

Nevertheless, Abraham felt bad that Hagar was treating Sarah rudely, so he said, "All right, Hagar is your servant, Sarah, and you can do whatever you want with her."

So Sarah started treating Hagar harshly. Hagar in turn ran away from Sarah (Genesis 16:6, 1 Peter 3:7). Hagar ran toward the Shur Desert and stopped at a spring to drink water, and while she was there, an angel of the Lord approached her and asked her, "Where have you come from and where are you going" (Genesis 16:7, Exodus 15:22)?

Hagar answered, "I am running away from my owner, Sarah."

The angel of the Lord said,

> Hagar, go back and be with Sarah [Titus 2:9]. I will give you a son called Ishmael because I have heard you cry for help. And later I will give you so many descendants that no one will be able to count them all [Exodus 3:7, Luke 1:13]. And your son Ishmael will live far away from his family. He will be like a wild donkey, fighting everyone, and everyone fighting him. (Genesis 16:8–9, 11–12)

Hagar was trying to run away from Sarah, but God would not let her. It was not her time. What I find interesting is that the angel of God prophesied about Hagar's son, who was not born yet. Hagar's son would be named Ishmael and separated from his family and a wild donkey fighting everyone. Ishmael does not know what is planned for him, born into a situation he has no control over. He will be separated from his father, Abraham.

Hagar thought she saw God, and from that day forward, she called God "The God Who Sees Me" (Genesis 16:13). Today people call the well between Kadesh and Bered the "Living One Who Sees Me" (Genesis 16:14). Abraham was eighty-six years old when Ishmael was born (Genesis 16:15, Galatians 4:22)

In terms of Hagar, Sarah's servant, she had no choice in this situation. She was told by her owner, Sarah, to be with her husband, Abraham. She became the second wife, which was customary in those days. But a big mistake! She trusted and believed in the angel of the Lord. That is what kept her motivated to serve. God knows everything. Can you see how God works? He is the same today as he was back in Sarah and Abraham's days. He has our life planned out if we are believers.

Abraham, Sarah, and Hagar received consequences. It is wise to think and pray about any relationships you have. Ask God to help you make the right decisions and wait for an answer. Some women get caught up in selfish affairs, and the children are the ones that suffer. Sarah and Abraham looked at satisfying their flesh, their own needs, without praying and bringing the problem to God. Until the next time.

Love,
Grandma

Grandkids

Seventeenth Chapter Letter

God's Promise to Abraham

Dear, grandkids. I hope all is well. Today is Thursday, May 21, 2020. In this letter, I will share what happened in Genesis, chapter 17, and how Moses writes about God's promise to Abraham. God told Abraham that he would be a father of many nations if he obeyed him and would have many descendants, and no one would be able to count them. In this chapter, God changed Abram's name to Abraham (Genesis 17:5) and Sarai's to Sarah (Genesis 17:15).

"Abraham was 99 years old when God appeared to him a second time and said, '*I am the God All-Powerful*'" (Genesis 17:1, Exodus 6:3, Deuteronomy18:13). God said to Abraham, "I will keep my solemn promise to you and give you more descendants than can be counted" (Genesis 17:2, Galatians 3:17). Abraham bowed down with his face to the ground, and God said, "I promise that you will be the father of many nations." Therefore, God changed his name to Abraham (Genesis 17:3–5, 1 Chronicles 1:27, Nehemiah 9:7, Romans 9:7). God told Abraham that he would give him a lot of descendants, and in the future, they will become great nations, and some will be kings (Genesis 17:6).

God promised Abraham and his descendants that he would take care of them because he is their God. "I will give you and them the land in which you are now a foreigner. I will give the land of Canaan to your family forever, and I will be their God" (Genesis 17:7–8, Galatians 3:17, Acts 7:5). God told Abraham, "You and all your future family must promise to obey me" (Genesis 17:9). And as a sign, Abraham pledged to God that he and all the males in his family and servants would be circumcised (Genesis 17:10–11, John 7:22, Exodus 12:48). God trusted and knew Abraham was obedient. Circumcision was a covenant/promise between God and Abraham. It was a clean start between them and everyone who was circumcised, a sign to others that Abraham and his descendants were dedicated to God. God said "every baby boy eight years old had to be circumcised," and whoever was not circumcised and did not keep God's promises was not one of God's people (Genesis 17:12–14, Leviticus 12:3, Exodus 12:14).

God told Abraham that his wife's name Sarai would be changed to Sarah and that he would bless her with a son and that she will become the mother of nations and even her descendants will be kings. "Abraham bowed his face to the ground and thought, 'I am almost 100 years old, and how can I become a father? And Sarah is 90, and how can she have a child?'" Abraham laughed.

Not sure why Abraham laughed; he must have forgotten his dad, Terah, was old when Abraham was born. He was 130 years old.

Abraham asked God, "Why not let Ishmael inherit what you have promised me" (Genesis 17:15–19, Galatians 4:28, Luke 3:34)? God said no! Abraham was concerned that Ishmael might be left out of his inheritance.

God told Abraham, "You and Sarah will have a son. His name will be Isaac, and I will make him and his descendants a promise" (Genesis 17:19, 11:24, 26; Luke 3:34). God knew what Abraham was thinking regarding his son Ishmael. God told Abraham that he would bless Ishmael and give him many descendants. Ishmael will be the father of twelve princes, and his family will be a great nation (Genesis 17:20–21).

Abraham showed concern for Ishmael's future. He wanted to make sure he was going to be taken care of. Thus, God promised Abraham that Ishmael would be okay because he will have a nation and many descendants. He eventually formed the Ishmaelites, who were Arab tribes.

Moreover, God told Abraham that Isaac would be born one year from that time, and the same promise made to Abraham would be made to Isaac and his family (Genesis 17:22). After God finished speaking to Abraham, he left. And that same day, Abraham obeyed God and circumcised Ishmael and all the males in the home, including himself. Abraham was ninety-nine years old, and his son Ishmael was thirteen (Genesis 17:23–27, Romans 4:11).

God is telling us, "*I am the God All-Powerful.*" He is the Creator. He changed Abram's name, which meant "High Father," to Abraham, suggesting that he will be the father of a multitude. Until the next time.

Love,
Grandma

Eighteenth Chapter Letter

Three Angels Visited Abraham

Greeting, grandkids. Today is Saturday, June 6, 2020, and people from all around the world from different backgrounds are protesting the murder of George Floyd, a forty-six-year-old Black man. It has been eleven straight days of protesting. The murder took place on May 25, 2020, in Minneapolis. A White officer handcuffed Mr. Floyd and put his body and face flat on the street with his knee on his neck for nine minutes and twenty-nine seconds, cutting off George Floyd's oxygen. I hope and pray God brings change to the world. Too many police officers are getting away with murdering people of color. Please be careful.

In chapter 18, in the book of Genesis, Moses writes about three angels visiting Abraham, and one of them was the Lord. These three angels were regular men, but Abraham knew they were special men. In this chapter, God promises Sarah and Abraham that they would have a son. Toward the middle of the chapter, God told Abraham what he planned to do with the city of Sodom and Gomorrah. God and Abraham had such an excellent and honest relationship. Abraham felt so comfortable with God that he tried to negotiate with him several times regarding saving people from Sodom and Gomorrah. Interesting dialog between the two.

It was a hot summer day when Abraham was sitting outside by the entrance of his tent near the sacred trees of Mamre when the Lord appeared to him (Genesis 18:1). "Abraham looked up and saw three men standing nearby. He immediately ran to meet them, bowed his face to the ground, and said, 'Please come to my home where I can serve you.'" Abraham had water to wash their feet, and they rested under the tree (Genesis 18:2–4). Abraham told the three angels that he would gather some food to build up their strength before they got ready to leave. Abraham knew they were important men. He said, "I would be an honor to serve you" (Genesis 18:5).

The three angels said, "Thank you, we will accept your offer."

Abraham ran to his tent and asked his wife Sarah to hurry up, get a large sack of flour, and make some bread. He quickly ran off to his herd of cattle and picked out one of the best calves and had his servants prepare a meal. Abraham served the angels yogurt, milk, and meat. He stood near and observed them while they were eating under the tree. They asked where his wife Sarah was. Abraham answered and said she was in the tent (Genesis 18:6–9).

One of the angels was the Lord, and he said, "I'll come back this time next year, and when I do, Sarah will already have a son."

Sarah was near Abraham by the entrance of the tent, listening. Sarah and Abraham were ancient. "Sarah felt she was too old to have any children. She laughed and said to herself, 'Now that I am old and worn out and my husband is old, will I know such happiness'" (Genesis 18:10–12, 2Kings 4:16).

God knew what Sarah was thinking and asked Abraham, "Why did Sarah laugh? Does Sarah doubt that she can have a child in her old age? I am the Lord! There is nothing too difficult for me" (Genesis 18:13–14, Numbers 11:23, Jeremiah 32:17). When he would come back the next year, God promised she would already have her son (Romans 9:9). Sarah was so afraid that she lied and said that "she didn't laugh." God knew what she was thinking to herself (Genesis 18:15, Psalm 63:11, Matthew 12:25). God knows everything. Always remember that.

Abraham Talks to God about the City of Sodom

When the three angels were getting ready to leave, Abraham walked part of the way with them. They stopped and looked down toward Sodom. The Lord thought to himself,

> I should tell Abraham what I am planning to do since I did promise him and his family that they will become a great and powerful nation and be a blessing to all other nations on earth. I have chosen him to teach his family to obey me forever and do what is right, and I have promised him many descendants. I need to tell Abraham what I heard the people from Sodom and Gomorrah are doing, all kinds of evil things. (Genesis 18:16–21, John 15:15, Romans 15:24)

God wanted to see if the people were terrible, and if they were not, he wanted to know.

The two men started walking toward Sodom while the Lord stayed back with Abraham. Abraham and God were hanging out on top of a hill, looking down at the city of Sodom.

Abraham asked the Lord, "When you destroy the evil people are you going to destroy the good people" (Genesis 18:22–23; Deuteronomy 4:9, 8:2; Acts 3:25). God listened. Abraham again asked the Lord if he would spare the city if fifty good people were living. Abraham said, "I know, Lord, you surely wouldn't let them be killed when you destroy the evil ones."

Again God just listened. Abraham was doing most of the talking. All along, God knew what he was thinking and going to say before he said it.

Abraham said, "Lord, you are the judge of all earth, and you do what is right."

The Lord answered, "If I find 50 good people in Sodom, I will save the city and keep them from being killed" (Genesis 18:24–26, Jeremiah 5:1).

Abraham continued talking, saying, "I am nothing more than the dust of the earth. Please forgive me, Lord, for daring to speak to you like this, but suppose there are 45 good people in Sodom, would you still wipe out the whole city" (Genesis 18:27–28)?

The Lord answered, "If I find 45 good people, I won't destroy the city."

Abraham said, "Lord, how about if there were 40 good people?"

The Lord said, "I would not destroy the city."

Abraham felt so comfortable talking to the Lord; he once again asked God not to be angry at him because he continued to ask, if thirty good people lived there, would he destroy the city.

The Lord said, "If I find 30 good people, I won't destroy it."

Abraham said, "Lord, I know I have no right to ask you, again, but if there were 20 good people?"

The Lord said, "Because of them, I won't destroy the city" (Genesis 18:29–31, 1 Thessalonians 5:17).

Finally, Abraham said, "Please do not get angry, Lord, if I speak just one more time. Suppose you find only ten good people there?"

The Lord said, "For the sake of the ten good people, I still won't destroy the city." Shortly after Abraham stopped asking questions, the Lord left, and Abraham went home (Genesis 18:32–33, Judges 6:39).

Abraham was genuinely nice to the three angels. He had a good idea they were godly people. The Lord did identify himself, which was beautiful. We will never know when we are entertaining angels (Hebrews 13:2). Always be kind to people. Abraham did most of the talking during his interaction with God. God knew what he was going to say beforehand, and he listened. God did inform Abraham he wanted to know what was going on in the city of Sodom. God was willing to spare the city if there were good people in it, but God knew they were not. He knows when we sin. "For the wages of sin is death, but the gift of God is enteral life in Christ Jesus our Lord" (Romans 6:23). Abraham knew his nephew Lot lived in that city and wanted to know if God would destroy him. In the following chapter letter, Lot is removed and saved before the town was destroyed. Lot was the only good person in that city.

Our Lord is a good God. We can pray, and he will listen as he did with Abraham. In terms of Sarah, doubting that she was too old to have a child showed her lack of faith. She also showed guilt when she lied. When you do wrong, the Holy Spirit that lives inside you will always let you know when you are guilty, just like he did with Sarah. Until next time.

Love,
Grandma

Nineteenth Chapter Letter

The City of Sodom and Gomorrah

Good morning, my beautiful grandkids. It has been a long time since I have written you. Today is Thursday, July 23, 2020. Our world is still in a crisis with the coronavirus. Millions of people are dying around the world because of this virus. I am convinced the Lord is trying to send a message to all of us on earth. We will know once this virus is over. There have been a lot of changes in our world because of this coronavirus. Yet God said to rejoice in times of tribulation (Romans 5:3).

I am at work today. I thank God that he has given me this opportunity to write to you while at work. It is slow right now on the job.

In Genesis 19, I will be writing about men who lived in Sodom and Gomorrah who liked having sex with young boys and men. These men were attracted to their gender. I say this is because in Genesis 19:4, Lot and God's angels were at Lot's home, and it was getting late when they heard knocking on the front door. The men who lived in the city of Sodom asked Lot to let them come in to get to know his guests, to have sex with them. Lot begged them to stop and to take his two daughters who had never been married. They refused!

The end of the chapter continues with God destroying the city of Sodom and Gomorrah, along with Lot's wife getting left behind because she did not obey God. The last part of the chapter talks about Lot's two daughters getting him drunk to sleep with him to have children.

The story begins with two of God's angels going to the city of Sodom to investigate the corruption. God already knew what was going on in terms of the men having sexual relationships with other men, and I am almost sure Lot knew as well. However, as the angels arrived, they saw Lot sitting near the entrance gate of the city of Sodom, which may indicate he is some type of leader in town (Genesis 19:1, Hebrews 13:2).

When Lot saw the angels, he immediately jumped on his feet and bowed his head, and said, "Gentlemen, I am your servant. Please come to my house where you can wash your feet, spend the night and be on your way tomorrow morning" (Genesis 19:2).

The angels answered, "No, we'll spend the night at the city square" (Genesis 19:3, Exodus 12:8).

Lot refused to accept no for an answer. He insisted they come to his home, so they said yes and went home with Lot. Lot made bread, cooked them a meal, and they ate. Again I think Lot knew evil men lived in the city and were nonbelievers who like having sex with men.

Shortly after they had dinner, it was getting dark when the men from Sodom knocked on Lot's front door, asking if they could come in to meet his guest so they could have sex with them (Genesis 19:4, Isaiah 47:15). They were young and older men standing outside Lot's front door, shouting for the angels to come out.

The men called out, "Where are your visitors" (Genesis 19:5, Isaiah 3:9)?

Lot came out of his front door and shut the door behind him. He said to the men, "Friends, please don't do such a terrible thing! I have two daughters who have never been married. I will bring them out to you! And you can do whatever you want with them just don't harm these men. They are my guests" (Genesis 19:6–8, Malachi 2:17).

The men became angry and upset with Lot. They told him, "Don't get in our way, and you're an outsider; what right do you have to order us around" (Genesis 19:9)? The men keep arguing and threatening Lot. They told Lot, "We will do worse things to you than we're going to do with them" (Genesis 19:9, Exodus 2:14, 2 Peter 2:7–8). The men of Sodom tried breaking the door down to get to the angels of God. But the two angels reached out their hands and pulled Lot back into his home. The angels blinded every man that was outside in the crowd trying to come in. They could not find the door to come in (Genesis 19:10–11).

The angels told Lot that the Lord had heard terrible things about the people of Sodom, and he had sent them to destroy the city. The angels ordered Lot to take his family and leave. He was to take all relatives, his daughters, and the men they were going to marry (Genesis 19:12–13, 2 Peter 2:7). Lot told his daughter's boyfriends that they had to hurry and leave because God was getting ready to destroy the city. They thought it was a joke and laughed at Lot (Genesis 19:14, Luke 17:28). The following day, the angels told Lot they had to leave the city immediately, or they would get swept away. Lot and his family were taking their time. The angels grabbed Lot's hand, his wife, and daughters and rushed them out of the city (Genesis 19:15–16, Luke 18:13, Psalm 34:22, Revelation 18:4).

When they were all finally out of the town, one of the angels said, "Run for your lives! And do not look back or stop anywhere in the valley or you will get swept away. Run to the mountain" (Genesis 19:17)!

As they were running away from the city, Lot thanked the angels for saving their lives. And at that moment, he asked the angels if he and his family could run to a small village nearby instead of the mountain because he felt they would die in the mountain. The angels said yes! The angels did not destroy the city of Sodom and Gomorrah, nor the small town nearby called Bela until Lot and his family were safe in the small village he requested to go. That small village is called Zoar, which means a tiny place (Genesis 19:18–2).

Lot and his family reached the small village just as the sun was coming down over the hills. Right at the time, the Lord had burning sulfur rain down from the sky, killing all the people and some of the plants and shrubs. Lot's wife turned around as she was following Lot and immediately turned into a pillar of salt (Genesis 19:23–26, Deuteronomy 29:23, Psalm 107:34). Unfortunately, it was too late to save her. The angels had warned Lot's family not to turn back while they were running away from Sodom. But his wife, not listening, died.

At the beginning of the story, Moses writes how God is against homosexuality. It is a sin (Leviticus 22:20, 1 Corinthians 6:9, Luke 17:34–37). He would rather see a man and woman together, not women and women or men and men. Millions of people on this earth today are gay, yet they are still our brothers and sisters. All we can do is love them and hope they can see the light of having a husband or wife with beautiful children one day.

The men from Sodom and Gomorrah seem like they were desperate to get their hands on God's angels to have sex with them. The story also shared how there were young boys and older men who were engaging in sex. When older men have sex with young boys, it is called a pedophilia. It is because they are attracted to children or small boys. These types of sexual behaviors are sinful.

In terms of Lot's wife, she should not have turned back. I believe she was thinking about the wealth they were leaving behind. I believe Lot was also thinking about his wealth in the back of his mind, but he knew not to look back. Lot's wife, on the other hand, forgot what the angels had said early not to look back. Lot was wealthy and greedy. They lived and associated themselves with evil people who refused to believe and know God. I have always said, *you are who you associate yourselves with.* You must be incredibly careful to choose who you hang around. Lot's wife knew she was leaving behind goods, and I think she hated to let it go. I understand her completely. After twenty years, I had to sell all my cars and rental properties to keep up my lifestyle after closing my business. I felt powerless, not able to spend money or buy what I wanted when I wanted. It was not a good feeling. I am at peace now and satisfied with what God has blessed me with. I have my health, plenty of food, and snacks in the cabinets for my grandkids; that is all that matters. God had once allowed me to experience having lots of material things that seemed important to me back then. But they are material things of the world. Now I have grace, peace, and love for all people.

Remember the last conversation God had with Abraham in terms of saving Sodom and Gomorrah. Abraham asked God if "ten good people lived in Sodom would you destroy it" (Genesis 18:32). God said if there were ten good people, he would save the city. But there were no good people! So God promised Abraham he would protect Lot before destroying the city of Sodom (Genesis 19:29).

God knew Abraham had concern for the safety of his nephew Lot, that is why he removed Lot from the city before he destroyed it. Prayer is powerful. I believe Abraham constantly prayed for Lot. He knew Lot was living and associating himself with evil people. But prayer saved him through the grace of God.

Lot and His daughters

Lot and his two daughters left the small village they lived in for a short time. They did not want to live in the same community because they were afraid of the people there. He moved to the cave the angel tried to get him to run to. The daughters realized they were the only ones left in their family and that their father was old and there was no one he could get to marry them (Genesis 19:30–31, Matthew 14:30). And because of that, they decided to get their father drunk with wine to have sex with him so they could have children (Genesis 19:32, Mark 12:19). When Lot was asleep, his oldest daughter had sex with him. He was so drunk he did not know it was his daughter (Genesis 19:33).

The next night, the youngest sister got Lot drunk and had sex with him. Unfortunately, he was too drunk to know it was his daughter (Genesis 19:34–35). The two sisters had children by their father, the first incest in a Bible story. Incest is sexual relations with a biological brother, sister, father, mother, and child. This type of behavior makes me wonder if these two sisters saw or learned it was okay from their home community in Sodom.

The oldest daughter named her son Moab, and he is the ancestor of the Moabites. The younger sister named her son Benammi, and he is the ancestor of the Ammonites (Genesis 19:36–38, Deuteronomy 2:19, Numbers 21:24). They were the descendants of Lot.

The book of Luke, chapter 17 verses 26–32, describes what to expect when there is constant sinning in the world. Jesus talked to his disciples and said, "When the son of man comes, things will be just as they were when Noah lived. People were eating, drinking, and getting married right up to when Noah went into the big boat. Then the flood came and drowned everyone on earth" (Luke 17:26–27).

Where Lot lived, people were also eating and drinking. They were buying, selling, planting, and building (Luke 17:28).

> But on the very day Lot left Sodom, fiery flames poured down from the sky and killed everyone. The same will happen on the day when the son of man appears. At that time, no one on a rooftop should go down into the house to get anything. No one in a field should go back to the house for anything. (Luke 17:29–31)

Remember what happened to Lot (Luke 17:32). These are potent verses. Please be aware of your surroundings, people you hang out with, and be careful how you behave in front of people. Treat people with love and respect, always. Until next time.

Love,
Grandma

Twentieth Chapter Letter

Abraham and Sarah at Gerar

Greetings, grandkids. I hope you all are doing well. Today is Thursday, August 6, 2020. I am at work. It is a slow day, so I decided to pick up where I left off. Our world is still in a crisis with the coronavirus. So far, there have been over 154,000 people who have died because of the virus. I thank God no one in our immediate family has gotten sick from the disease.

In chapter 20 of Genesis, Abraham moved to the southern desert, where he and his family settled between Kadesh and Shur before moving to Gerar. Before he arrived in Gerar, he told everyone to say Sarah was his sister. He was worried that the king from Gerar would like Sarah and take her for one of his wives (Genesis 20:1–2). Here Abraham showed fear and lied again. In the twelfth letter, Abraham went into Egypt and told Sarah to lie to Pharaoh and say she was his sister. Thus, Abraham had lied twice regarding his wife, Sarah. Again he lost focus instead of trusting God to help him. If we stay in prayer, we will never worry about a situation because we will know God is with us.

When Abraham settled in Gerar, King Abimelech requested to have Sarah brought to him. God knew what was taking place and immediately came to Abimelech in a dream and said, "You have taken a married woman, and for this, you will die" (Genesis 20:3 Psalm 105:14). King Abimelech was frightened. He asked God not to kill him and said, "I haven't slept with Sarah." He continued, saying,

"They told me they were brother and sister." He felt it was not his fault. He told God he was innocent (Genesis 20:4–5, Deuteronomy 32:4). God came to Abimelech in another dream and told him he knew he was innocent, so that was why he kept him from sleeping with Sarah. He told the king that Abraham was a prophet and to return Sarah to Abraham and that his life would be saved because Abraham would pray for him (Genesis 20:6–7; Leviticus 6:2; 1 Samuel 25:26, 1 Samuel 7:5).

The following morning, the king shared with his officials what had happened, and they were afraid. King Abimelech then sent for Abraham and told him, "Look what you have done to us! What have I ever done to you? Why did you make me and my nation guilty of such terrible sin?" (Genesis 20:8–10).

Abraham said, "I didn't think any of you would respect God. And I thought you would kill me for my wife Sarah" (Genesis 20:11). Abraham told the king that Sarah was his half-sister and had the same father but different mothers. "When God made me leave my father's home and wander, I told Sarah, if she loved me, she would tell everyone that I was her brother" (Genesis 20:12–13, Hebrews 11:8).

Sarah was a beautiful woman. Abraham was afraid and did not want to lose her. So he lied and forgot about his faith. There is no need to lie when you are faced with fear. Be honest, even if you think you should not be.

King Abimelech was relieved about the situation. He gave Abraham sheep, cattle, and servants. He sent Sarah back to Abraham and told him he could "settle anywhere in this country." And he told Sarah that he gave Abraham, her brother, thousands of pieces of silver as proof to everyone she did not do anything wrong (Genesis 20:14–5). No one did anything wrong. Abraham assumed the king was going to be disrespectful and take his wife, Sarah. He should be honest, tell the truth, admit Sarah was his wife, and trust that God had his hand in the situation. Sometimes we make things worse in our lives instead of relying on the process. Go with your gut feeling, your spirit!

The king said, "What did I ever do to you?" There will be times when we are tested. The goal is to be honest. The king was humble, and God blessed him, Abimelech, his wife, and servants with children (Genesis 20:16–18). Until the next time.

Love,
Grandma

Twenty-First Chapter Letter

Sarah and Her Son, Isaac

Hello, grandkids. Today is Sunday, December 13, 2020. It has been four months since the last letter I have written you. So much has happened. The deadly coronavirus is still killing millions of people on earth. The state governments are shutting down dine-in restaurants, nail shops, gyms, and many other businesses worldwide, including churches. I feel like I am in a dream. Everyone must wear a mask when they are in public and at work. It does not feel normal. God is still in control of his world. All I can do is trust him and know he has our back. He has his reasons for allowing this virus to go on. I am not going to try to figure it out. Solomon said "it's like chasing the wind," which you will never catch. In the book of Ecclesiastes, Solomon describes what the meaning of life is. It is an excellent book to read!

I have been working days and taking care of your grandma Josie who has Alzheimer's. The disease has increased. Thank you, Little Marvin and Daniel, for helping with Grandma Josie. Our aunt Lola passed away on December 6 from Alzheimer's. This disease is not inherited, so do not worry about it.

In this letter, I will be sharing with you what happened in Genesis 21. From chapters 21 to 26, I will write to you about Isaac's life. In this chapter story, Isaac was born. Sarah chased off her Egyptian servant, Hagar, because she was jealous of her. However, God's angel comforted the Egyptian woman while she was in the desert. The story ends with Abraham making a promise to a king named Abimelech. I want to point out that Ishmael was born from the desires of the flesh and Isaac, from the spirit. The flesh is of this world. The Spirit is from God. Remember, I wrote the story in letter 16 describing how Sarah allowed Abraham to marry her servant because she wanted a son, Sarah's desires of the flesh, not God's will at that time.

Our Lord God kept his promise to Sarah regarding having a baby boy (Genesis 17:21, 18:10). Abraham was very old when Sarah had a son, when God told her she would have it (Genesis 21:1–2). Abraham named their son Isaac which means "he or one that laughs," When he turned eight days old, he was circumcised, just as God told Abraham he must do to all males (Genesis 21:3–4, Acts 7:8–9). Abraham was one hundred years old when Isaac was born, and Sarah could not believe she had a baby boy. She said, "God has made me laugh, now everyone will laugh with me." (Genesis 21:5–6, Luke 1:58). Isn't it interesting that Isaac's name means "he laughs"? Do you see, grandkids, how things happen in life? There are no accidents in life, and things happen for a reason. God sets it up to his way.

Sarah could not believe she had a child at their old age. She said, "Who would have told Abraham that I would give him a child in his old age" (Genesis 21:7). When their son, Isaac, grew up and did not have to be nursed, Abraham made a big feast that same day (Genesis 21:8; 1 Kings 8:65).

Hagar and Ishmael Are Sent Away

One day, Sarah saw Hagar's son Ishmael being disrespectful and mocking her, and she disapproved (Genesis 21:9, Galatians 4:29), and because of that, Sarah told Abraham to send her away. Sarah said to Abraham, "I don't want this Egyptian woman and her son here; get rid of them" (Genesis 21:10). Abraham was concerned and worried about their safety, and God knew that (Genesis 21:11). God told Abraham, "Do not worry about your servant and her son; they will be alright. Do what Sarah has asked you to do" (Genesis 21:12, Matthew 1:2). God also told Abraham, "Ishmael is also your son, and he will inherit your family name, and I will make his descendants into a great nation" (Genesis 21:13).

Early the following morning, Abraham told Hagar she had to leave and helped her pack up. He gave her an animal skin full of water and some bread, put Ishmael on her shoulder, and sent them away. They wandered around Beersheba (Genesis 21:14, John 8:35). When they ran out of water, Hagar put her son under a bush (Genesis 21:15). Hagar could not witness her son suffer and die because of no water and food. She went away from him so that she could not hear him cry. God heard her crying terribly (Genesis 21:16). When God heard the boy crying, the angels of God called out to Hagar from heaven and said, "Hagar, why are you worried? Why are you afraid? I have heard your son crying, go help him up and hold him because I am going to make him the father of a great nation" (Genesis 21:17–18, Exodus 3:7). God prophesied, promised Hagar that her son would not be left out of any inheritance; God had his back!

God let Hagar see a well full of water. She filled her animal skin with water and gave some to her son (Genesis 21:19, Numbers 22:31, Genesis 16:7). God blessed Ishmael as he grew older; he became an expert with the bow and arrows. He lived in the Paran Desert. His mother chose him an Egyptian woman to marry (Genesis 21:20–21). I am sure they felt abandoned by Abraham. Hagar was a single mom, but she trusted God would see her through. Have you ever been kicked out of your home by one parent and felt like you were mistreated? Dysfunctional families are nothing new in this world. It is typical today in our culture for parents to divorce or separate and take one or two children with her or him. Separation of families will bring on stress for any parent or child. In Hagar's case, she reached out to God for help, and he saw her through her difficult times. God is our father, and he will take care of us if you trust and believe in him! He will see you through your pain and family issues.

Abimelech and Abraham Made Peace

Abimelech and his army commander, Phicol, I think, thought about their relationship with Abraham and wanted to make peace with Abraham. They could see God's hands working in Abraham's life, and they were afraid. Abimelech said, "Abraham, God blessed you with everything you do, and because of that, I want you to promise me in the name of God you will always be loyal to me and my descendants, just as I have been good to you in this land where you have been living as a foreigner" (Genesis 21:22–24). Abraham agreed!

I find it interesting that the king wanted to make peace; he either had something up his sleeve or worried about Abraham's God. It seems to me that King Abimelech would like to know who Abraham's God was so that he could get the same blessings Abraham was receiving.

Abimelech witnessed how God operated in Abraham's life. Abraham was full of grace, a humble and faithful man who had a close relationship with God, and he was blessed. When people are humble and kind, it is easy to see God's light shine upon them. Having a close relationship with our Lord Jesus Christ will give you grace and peace, and you can be a reflection of God's love.

One day, Abraham told Abimelech that one of his servants took over one of his wells of waters. Abimelech said, "This was the first time I have heard of this complaint. Why didn't you say something beforehand? I don't have any idea who did it" (Genesis 21:25–26). Because Abraham wanted to make peace with Abimelech, he gave him sheep and cattle (Genesis 21:27). In addition, he separated seven female lambs from his flock of sheep. Abimelech asked Abraham, "'Why are you doing this?' Abraham replied, "Please accept the seven lambs as proof I dug the well'" (Genesis 21:28–30). And because Abimelech agreed, they made peace at that point and called it Beersheba (Genesis 21:31).

Shortly after, Abimelech and his army commander Phicol went back to the land of the Philistines (Genesis 21:32), and Abraham planted a tamarisk tree in Beersheba and worshiped the Lord God there. "Abraham lived a long time as a foreigner in that land of the Philistines" (Genesis 21:33–34). This story had a great ending. It is best to make peace with your neighbors. Until next time.

Love,
Grandma

Twenty-Second Chapter Letter

The Lord Tells Abraham to Offer Isaac as a Sacrifice

Greetings, my beloved grandkids. I hope you are in a good place in your life. Today is Friday, January 8, 2021, my first letter to you this year. I am currently not working. I am getting ready to move in with your great-grandma Josie. Her Alzheimer's/dementia is getting worse. It breaks my heart to see her mental status declining. She was a powerful and independent woman at one time, and to see her not remember things is hurtful. God bless her!

In this letter, I will be sharing the story of what happens in Genesis, chapter 22, how God tested Abraham by using his son Isaac. The story ends with Abraham's brother Nahor getting married and having eight sons.

Years had passed when God spoke to Abraham. Abraham answered God and said, "Here I am." Our God told Abraham to get his only son, the one he loved dearly, and take him to a land called Moriah where there is a mountain, and he would be sacrificing his son on an altar (Genesis 22:1–2, James 1:12, 1 Peter 1:7, Hebrews 11:17, John 5:20).

In this Bible verse, God spoke of Abraham's *only spiritual son* he blessed him and Sarah with; Abraham's first son was named Ishmael with Sarah's Egyptian servant named Hagar (Genesis 16:3). Ishmael was born first, naturally, whereas Isaac was born with God's blessings.

God planned and blessed Sarah and Abraham with Isaac in their old age (Genesis 21:2), whereas Ismael was out of selfish desires, without God's blessings.

The following day, Abraham woke up early and chopped wood for the fire. He got his donkey ready by putting a saddle on it, his son, Isaac, and gathered two of his servants to travel with them (Genesis 22:3). Three days later, Abraham looked off the distance and saw the place. He told his servants to stay with the donkey while "my son and I go over and worship. We will be right back" (Genesis 22:4–5, Hebrews 11:19). Abraham put the wood on Isaac's shoulder, and he carried the hot coals and knife while they were walking. Isaac said, "Father, we have the coals and wood. Where is the lamb that will be sacrificed?" Abraham answered, "My son, God will provide the lamb," and they continued to walk (Genesis 22:6–8, John 19:17, John 1:29). Abraham was talking about Jesus. He prophesied Jesus would be carrying the cross.

When Abraham and his son Isaac reached the place where God told him to sacrifice his son, he built an altar and placed the wood on it, tied up his son, laid him on the wood (Genesis 22:9, Hebrews 11:17, James 2:21). Abraham pulled out his knife and got ready to kill his son. Right at that moment, God's angel shouted from heaven, "'Abraham! Abraham!' Abraham answered, 'Here I am'" (Genesis 22:10–11). God's angel said, "Don't hurt the boy. Now I know that you truly obeyed God and were willing to offer your son, your only son" (Genesis 22:12, 1 Samuel 15:22). The Bible does not mention how old Isaac was when this incident happened.

Our heavenly Father tested Abraham's faith, and he passed with flying colors. Abraham believed if he had to kill his only son God blessed him and Sarah with, that he would raise him from the dead. And remember, God promised Abraham that through his descendants, he would have many nations and kings. Here is a clear example of Abraham's faith. I work hard every day to trust and have faith in the Lord like Abraham, but there is no way I could do what Abraham did with his son Isaac. Where is your trust and confidence in the Lord?

Right after the angel told Abraham to stop and not hurt his son, Abraham looked up and saw a ram caught by its horn in the bushes. Abraham took the ram and sacrificed it in place of his son. He named the area "The Lord Will Provide," and even today, when people see the mountain, it is called "The Lord Will Provide" (Genesis 22:13–14).

The Lord's angel called out to Abraham a second time and said,

> You were willing to offer your son to the Lord, and he made you a solemn promise. I will bless you and give you a large family, and someday your descendants will be more numerous than the stars in the sky or the grains of sand along the beach. They will defeat their enemies and take over the cities where their enemies live. You have obeyed me, and so you and your descendants will be a blessing to all nations on earth. (Genesis 22:15–18, Luke 1:73–74, Hebrews 6:13–14, Acts 3:25, Psalm 105:9)

Abraham and Isaac went back to where their servants were waiting, and they all returned to Beersheba (Genesis 22:19). What a beautiful ending to have angels from heaven talk to us. I am positively convinced if we sit still and listen to the Spirit that lives in us, we will hear our angel comfort and direct us too.

The Children of Nahor, Abraham's Brother

In the eleventh chapter letter, I mentioned Abraham's father, Terah, having three sons—Abraham, Nahor, and Haran. Abraham married his half-sister, Sarah, and his brother Nahor married his niece, Milcah. Haran was Lot and Milcah's father. I just wanted to remind you of Abraham's brothers.

Nahor and his wife Milcah had eight sons, and the following are the names of their sons: firstborn was Huz or Uz; second, Buz; and third Kemuel, who became the father of Aram (Genesis 22:20). The other five were Chesed, Hazo, Pildash, Jidlaph, and Bethuel, who became the father of Rebekah, or better known as Rebecca (Genesis 22:21–23, Job:32:2). Nahor also married his servant, and they had four sons: Tebah, Graham, Tahash, and Maacah (Genesis 22:24). Rebecca was chosen to marry Abraham's son Isaac. I will share their story in chapter letter 24. Until next time.

Love,
Grandma.

Twenty-Third Chapter Letter

Sarah's Death and Burial

Hello, my beautiful grandkids. I hope all is well with you. Today is Wednesday, January 13, 2021, and I am currently working on getting my nonprofit, Galvez Community Services, back up and running to help parents keep their children out of the foster care system and provide counseling for the families. It has been my passion. The problem is there has not been any money to support the nonprofit right now. In the meantime, I will continue caring for Grandma Josie. Her mind continues to decline, but the rest of the family is doing well. The coronavirus is still a significant issue in California. I still believe God is in control of his world and what is happening in it. I have faith that good will come out of this horrible experience we are all facing.

In this letter, I will be writing to you about what took place in Genesis, chapter 23. Sarah was 127 years old and died in Kiriath-Arba, known as Hebron, in the land of Canaan (Genesis 23:1–2, Joshua 14:15). Unfortunately, her son, Isaac, is not mentioned in this chapter. However, I will talk more about him in the following letters.

After Abraham mourned for her, he began looking for a place to bury her. He went to the Hittites and said, "I live as a foreigner in your land, and I don't own any property where I can bury my wife. Please allow me to buy a piece of land" (Genesis 23:3–4; Hebrews 11:9, 13; Acts 7:5).

They answered Abraham and said, "Sir, you are an important man. Choose the best place to bury your wife; none of us would refuse a place for your dead" (Genesis 23:5).

Abraham had a good reputation, and people knew he was a godly man. A good reputation will get you a long way. Always treat people with love and kindness as Abraham did.

Abraham was so humble he bowed down when he replied (Genesis 23:6). He said, "If you are willing to let me bury my wife here, please ask Zohar's son Ephron to sell me Machpelah Cave at the end of the field" (Genesis 23:7, Romans 13:7). Abraham was willing to pay anything to have a space to bury Sarah. Ephron was sitting nearby the city gate when he overheard Abraham's request.

Ephron told Abraham, "You are welcome to have the entire field, including the cave, and my people can be a witness to what I am saying. You can freely have a burial place for your dead" (Genesis 23:8–11, 2 Samuel 24:21–24). Abraham was so humble that he bowed his head again and told Ephron that he would pay whatever the land is worth.

Abraham said, "Please accept my offer" (Genesis 23:12–13).

Ephron answered, "The property is only worth four hundred pieces of silver." He did not want to hassle over the property, so he told Abraham it was his to take it! Abraham accepted it and paid him four hundred pieces of silver, and his people witnessed the transaction at the city gate (Genesis 23:14–16, Exodus 30:13, Jeremiah 32:9).

Abraham was happy with the deal. It was located east of Hebron, and it included the field with trees, and the Machpelah cave was located at the end of the area. Abraham buried Sarah in the cave he purchased from the Hittites (Genesis 23:17–20). Abraham did not own any land at this point in his life, and he was a rich man. Remember God promised Abraham that his descendants would be kings and have nations around the world. However, God did not say Abraham would. Until next time.

Love,
Grandma

Twenty-Fourth Chapter Letter

Abraham Finds a Wife
for His Son Isaac

Greetings, my sweet grandkids. I hope life is treating you well. Today is Sunday, January 24, 2021. There has been a lot going on since the last time I have written you. We have a new president in office, Joe Biden, and a vice president, Kamala Harris, the first African and Asian American woman. They took office on January 20, 2021. I am so excited for America. Hopefully, things will start changing for the better in terms of the virus and the economic status. People continue to die every day because there is not enough medicine to help people fight the virus. It is sad. Again I believe God is in control of everything.

Papa and I have remodeled Uncle Marvin's bathroom. It took us two months; it is big and beautiful. I am continuing to care for Grandma Josie. I had to move in with her because her mental health has gotten worse.

In Genesis, chapter 24, Moses writes how Abraham instructed one of his close and trusted employees to go back to his hometown where he was born and choose a wife for his son Isaac from his tribe. He did not want Isaac to marry anyone from the Canaan tribe. The story in this chapter is long. There are sixty-seven verses.

Abraham was old, wealthy, and successful at this point in his life (Genesis 24:1). God had blessed him tremendously. One day,

Abraham instructed his trusted servant to promise that he would not allow his son Isaac to marry anyone from the Canaan tribe. Abraham said, "Solemnly promise me in the name of the Lord, who rules heaven and earth that you will not choose a wife for my son Isaac from the people here in the land of Canaan" (Genesis 24:2–3, 1 Chronicles 29:24, Deuteronomy 7:3). In those days, the elders preferred that their people marry within their tribe and not marry others with different beliefs. There are some cultures today that feel the same way. For example, Middle Eastern culture would rather see their children marry within their culture. When my oldest son, Marvin, was born, I remember many Mexicans and Black people disapproved of it. But times have changed now. There are many mixed children, cultures, and religious backgrounds, and we all learn from each other. I think that is what makes the world so beautiful.

Abraham Sent His Servant to Find a Wife for Isaac

Abraham told his servant to go back to the land where he was born and find a wife from among his family. The servant said to Abraham, "What if the wife doesn't want to leave home or come back with me, and should I just take Isaac with me to look for a wife" (Genesis 24:4–5)?

Abraham said, "No, don't ever take him back there no matter what. The Lord who rules heaven brought me to the land where he promised me" (Genesis 24:6). Abraham did not want to leave the land where he was. He knew one day the land would go to his descendants.

Abraham told his servant to go back to his land where the Lord brought him out, and God will send his angel ahead to help him find a wife for Isaac (Genesis 24:7). Abraham said, "If the woman refuses to come along, you don't have to keep this promise. But do not ever take my son Isaac back there" (Genesis 24:8, Joshua 2:17). "The servant gave Abraham his word that he would do everything he asked" (Genesis 24:9). Abraham had great faith that God would send an angel to help his servant. It was clear that Abraham had prayed beforehand and asked God specifically what he wanted for his son, and God answered him.

To have faith like Abraham is humbling. Prayer is powerful, and God promises us that he will "never leave us nor forsake us" (Deuteronomy 31:6) if we stay faithful. Having faith like Abraham takes commitment and dedication. He had confidence that God had his back. Confidence that God is always holding our hands is a beautiful feeling. I must admit I forget the power we carry.

Shortly after Abraham instructed the servant on how and what to do regarding finding his son a wife, the servant loaded ten camels with valuable gifts. He headed out toward the city in northern Syria where Abraham's brother Nahor lived (Genesis 24:10). When they arrived late in the evening, the camels rested near the well outside the city. While the servant waited, he began to pray (Genesis 24:11). It was a custom for women to get water from the well throughout the day and evenings in those days.

The servant prayed to the Lord, "You are the God my master Abraham worships. Please keep your promise to him and let me find a wife for Isaac today" (Genesis 24:12). He believed that a young woman from the city would come by soon to get water from the well (Genesis 24:13, Exodus 2:16). He was waiting for one so that he could ask her for a drink of water. The servant knew if one of the women would give him a cup of water and offered some water to his camels, she would be the one God chose to be Isaac's wife and that the promise to Abraham was honored (Genesis 24:14, Judges 6:17). The servant had learned from observing Abraham worshiping the Lord that he also believed in Abraham's God. Modeling praying habits will send a powerful message to those watching, as it did with Abraham's servant. Teach your kids while they are young so they will remember to teach their kids. Do not ever be ashamed of the Lord.

The servant continued to pray for a beautiful unmarried woman. As he was praying, a woman walked by with a jar on her shoulder. Rebekah, the daughter of Bethuel—the son of Abraham's brother Nahor and his wife, Milcah—walked past the servant and went to the well to fill her water jar (Genesis 24:15–16, Isaiah 65:24).

The servant immediately ran to her and asked for some water. Rebekah said, "I will be glad to give you some water." She removed the jar from her shoulders and held it for him while he started drinking the water. After he finished drinking the water, Rebekah volunteered to give some water to his camels. She said they could have as much as they want (Genesis 24:17–20, 1 Peter 3:8–9). God chose Rebekah to be Isaac's wife. She was very humble and caring to Abraham's servant. She provided water to the servants and animals. You must treat everyone with respect and help others when needed, like Rebekah.

Abraham's servant observed everything that was going on. He did not say a word to Rebekah; he stood back and watched her. He wanted to make sure she was the one God had chosen for Isaac (Genesis 24:21). Recall the servant brings along expensive gifts for the woman, a gold ring and bracelets (Genesis 24:22, Isaiah 3:19–21). The servant observed her, and when she finished bringing water to the servants and camels, Abraham's servant gave her a ring for her nose and a bracelet for her arm. Next, the servant asked Rebekah, "Can you please tell me who your father is? Do you think your father has room for me and my men to spend the night" (Genesis 24:23)?

She answered, "My father, is Bethuel, the son of Nahor and Milcah. We have a place for you and your men to stay the night and enough straw to feed your camels" (Genesis 24:24).

The servant was so happy he could not speak! The servant bowed his head and prayed and thanked God for leading him to Abraham's relatives and keeping Abraham's promises (Genesis 24:25–27, Exodus 4:31). The servant was faithful and committed to Abraham. He prayed for his boss and trusted God would come through for Abraham. It is always kind to pray for other people, your boss, neighbors, and others you see that may need prayer.

Rebekah was so happy she ran home and shared with her family what happened (Genesis 24:28). Her brother Laban overheard her tell the family about the servant. He saw the ring and bracelets she was wearing and was excited for her. He ran out to see Abraham's servant standing by his camels at the well (Genesis 24:29–30). Laban immediately said to the servant, "The Lord has brought you safely here. Come home with me. There is no need for you to keep standing out here. I have a room for you in our home, and there is also a place for your camels" (Genesis 24:31, Judges 17:2).

Abraham's servant went with Laban to their home. Laban's servants unloaded his camels and fed them straw. They also gave Abraham's servants water to wash their feet (Genesis 24:32). Shortly, food was brought out to them. But Abraham's servant said,

> "Before I eat, I have to tell you why I have come." Laban said, "Go ahead and tell us." Abraham's servant said: "I am Abraham's servant. The Lord has been good to Abraham and has made him extraordinarily rich. He has many sheep, goats, cattle, camels, and donkeys, as well as a lot of silver and gold, and many servants. And Sarah, Abraham's wife, did not have any children until she was old. Then God blessed her with a son, and Abraham gave him everything. Abraham told me not to choose a wife for his son from the women in the land of Canaan. And I have solely promised Abraham that I would honor his request. He told me to come to his land where he was born and find a wife for his son from his relatives. Therefore I am here," said the servant. (Genesis 24:33–38, John 4:34)

The servant continued to share the conversation he had with Abraham. Finally, the servant said,

> I told Abraham, "What if the young woman refuses to come back with me?" Abraham answered, "I have always obeyed the Lord, and he will send his angel to help you find a wife for my son from my relatives And if the family refused to allow her to come back with you, then you are free from your responsibility." (Genesis 24:39–40)

Abraham's confidence in the Lord was so strong. He knew God would honor his wishes and find a wife for his son Isaac from his family. Grandkids, to have faith that strong is beautiful. Your trust for our Lord must be that strong. Know that God has your back no matter what! I cannot say that enough.

The servant told Laban that when he came to the well, he silently prayed, "Lord, you are the God of Abraham whom he worships, please lead me to a wife for his son while I am at the well. And when a woman comes out to get water, I will ask her to give me a drink. If she gives me a drink and offers to give some to my camels, I'll know she is the one you chose" (Genesis 24:41–44).

Even before the servant had finished praying, Rebekah walked by with a water jar on her shoulder. "When she had finished filling the jar, I asked her for a drink. Rebekah quickly lowered the jar from her shoulder and said, 'Have a drink. Then I'll get water for your camels.' So, I drank the water, and shortly after, Rebekah got some water for my camels" (Genesis 24:45–46, Isaiah 65:24).

Abraham's servant was so happy. He asked Rebekah who her father was, and she said, "Nahor and Micah." The servant knew immediately she was the right woman for Abraham's son, so he put the ring in her nose and the bracelets on her arm (Genesis 24:47). The servant was so honored that he quickly bowed his head and thanked the God Abraham worshiped. Then the Lord led him straight to Abraham's relatives and found Isaac's wife (Genesis 24:48). What an exciting beginning for Rebekah. God had this all planned out before the servant went back to Abraham's hometown. Moreover, this is how God works if we trust him! He has a plan for all of us; we must believe he is in control.

The servant asked the family,

> "Will your daughter do right by Abraham's son, or shall I look for another young woman." Laban and Bethuel said, "The Lord has done this. We have no choice in this situation. Feel free to take Rebekah with you. She can marry Abraham's

son, just as the Lord arranged." (Genesis 24:49–
51, Psalm 118:23, Matthew 21:42)

I cannot stress this enough that the Lord is in control. He told
me to get up and to write to my grandkids. He knew I was going to
be writing these letters to you! And whoever is reading these letters
is not an accident.

Abraham's servant was so honored that the family trusted
him and the Lord that he bowed down and thanked God (Genesis
24:52). The servant gave Rebekah clothing, silver, and gold jew-
elry. He gave her brother and mother gifts (Genesis 24:53, Exodus
3:22, 2 Chronicles 21:3). He and his men ate, drank, and spent the
night there. The following day, they got up, and the servant said to
Rebekah's mother and brother,

> "I would like to go back to see Abraham
> now." They said, "Let Rebekah stay with us for a
> week or ten days, then she may go with you." The
> servant replied, "Do not make me stay any lon-
> ger. The Lord has already helped me find a wife
> for Abraham's son; now, I must return." They
> answered, "Let's ask Rebekah what she wants to
> do." They called her in and asked her if she was
> willing to leave with the servant right now. She
> said, "Yes." (Genesis 24:54-58)

The family agreed to let Rebekah go. One of the family's servants was going with Rebekah. The family gave Rebekah their blessings and said, "We pray that God will give you many children and
grandchildren and that will help them defeat their enemies" (Genesis
24:59–60). God will never let anyone hurt you physically or ruin
what you have built. When God opens a door for you, man cannot
close it. I remember some tried to close my business, but God would
not let it happen. Instead, God said, "I will make your enemies your
footstool" (Luke 20:43).

Rebekah Leaves Her Family

Rebekah and her servant packed up their belongings and got on camels, left with Abraham's servant and his men (Genesis 24:61). During this time, Isaac lived in the southern part of Canaan near a place called "The Well of the Living One Who Sees Me" (Genesis 24:62). One evening, Isaac was walking out in the fields when he suddenly saw a group of people on camels walking his way. Rebekah saw Isaac walking her way, and she stopped and got off the camel. She asked who was this man. Abraham's servant said, "He is my boss." Rebekah immediately covered her face with her veil (Genesis 24:63–65). She knew this was the man she was going to marry. The servant told his boss everything that had happened. Isaac then asked Rebekah to come with him into the tent his mother used to live in before she died. Rebekah followed Isaac, and they married. Isaac loved Rebekah. "She comforted him over the loss of his mother" (Genesis 24:66–67). Grandkids, the timing was perfect. I do not believe in accidents. All things happen for a reason. Until the next time.

Love,
Grandma

Twenty-Fifth Chapter Letter

Abraham Marries Keturah, His Third Wife

Good morning, my sweet grandkids. I hope life has been treating you well. Today is Saturday, April 3, 2021, and it has not been easy living with Grandma Josie. Her dementia is worsening. I miss my home and husband, but I know this is temporary. When my mom forgets who I am, I will move her to my house. Tomorrow is Easter Sunday. We are all planning to meet up and celebrate Jesus's resurrection.

In this following letter, I will be writing about what happened in Genesis, chapter 25. Abraham married his third wife, a servant (1 Chronicles 1:32), and they had six sons, grandkids, and great-grandkids. In this chapter in the Bible, Abraham died. First, I will talk about Abraham's first son, Ishmael, and his twelve sons. Then I will write about Isaac meeting his new wife, Rebekah, and how they had twin boys named Esau and Jacob. The stories get more interesting as the characters get older.

Abraham and Keturah had six sons, their names were

- Zimran,
- Jokshan,
- Medan,
- Midian,

- Ishbak, and
- Shuah (Genesis 25:1–2).

Jokshan became the father of Sheba and Dedan (grandkids).

And when Dedan grew up, he had three sons (great-grandkids) named

- Asshurim,
- Letushim, and
- Leummim.

When Midian grew up, he had five sons (grandkids) named

- Ephah,
- Epher,
- Hanoch,
- Abida, and
- Eldaah (Genesis 25:3–4).

The descendants of Dan were the tribes of the Asshurites, the Letushites, and the Leumites. Out of six sons, Abraham and Keturah had seven grandkids and three great-grandkids. Abraham continued to care for his sons, Ishmael and the six sons he had with Keturah. He sent them gifts. However, Abraham did not want his son Isaac to grow up with Hagar and Keturah's sons, so he sent them to go live in the east, far from his son. It was God's plan for the stepbrothers to live separate lives because Ishmael was the ancestor of the Arabs, or the Ishmaelites, and his stepbrother Isaac was the ancestor of the Jew population.

Recall in chapter 17, God promised Abraham he would be the father of many nations (Genesis 17:4), and he promised Hagar that her son Ishmael would be the father of twelve princes and have his nation (Genesis 17:20–21). So Ishmael and these families were the Arabian tribes. The countries were starting to form. In the Quran (2:127), Abraham and Ishmael built the foundation of Ka'aba, a building or house located in Mecca, Saudia Arabia. It is where the Islamic religion started.

When Abraham died, he left everything to his son Isaac (Genesis 25:5–6, Judges 6:3). Abraham was 175 when he passed away. His two oldest sons, Isaac and Ishmael, buried him east of Hebron in the Machpelah Cave, part of the field Abraham had bought from Ephron, son of Zohar. God blessed Isaac after he buried his dad. He eventually moved to a place called "The Well of the Living One Who Sees Me" (Genesis 25:11).

Ishmael's Descendants

Ishmael was Abraham's first son from the Egyptian woman Hagar, Sarah's servant (Genesis 25:12). Ishmael had twelve sons, starting with the oldest: Nebaioth, Kedar, Adbeel, Mibsam, Mishma, Dumah, Massa, Hadad, Tema, Jetur, Naphish, and Kedemah (Genesis 25:13–15). "Each of Ishmael's sons was a tribal chief, and villages were named after them" (Genesis 25:16).

Recall in chapter 10, Moses outlined Noah's three sons, Shem, Ham, and Japheth. They had their languages, tribes, and nations that would be named after them. So when you are reading these foreign names, they are family members that stemmed from Noah's sons. I may say this to you several times to bring you back to where the world began populating.

Ishmael had settled in the land east of his brothers, and his sons settled everywhere from Havilah to Shur, east of Egypt on the way to Asshur. The name Asshur came from the son of Shem, who was Noah's oldest son. So the Assyrians are Semites and Shem's descendants.

Ishmael finally died at the age of 137 (Genesis 25:17–18, Samuel 15:7). The brothers fought against each other and formed their own beliefs regarding God. Some followed Christianity, others believed in the Jewish doctrine, and many leaned toward the Muslim culture. We are all family and related to each other, and no matter what you chose to believe in, we must not judge any person's beliefs. Abraham's descendants had their nations and villages named after themselves. God made a promise to Abraham that this would happen, and indeed it did.

Although the brothers lived in anger and bitterness toward each other, this problem started when Abraham married the Black Egyptian woman Hagar and had Ishmael. He was Abraham's first son from a servant, against God's will. Isaac was a blessing from God. Abraham and Sarah were old and wanted a son, and God blessed them with Isaac, which brought tension between the mothers and brothers because of different circumstances.

Moreover, it does not matter who was born first or second. And if your dad or mom have children from his or her first or second husband or wife. The point is, we must get along with our half-siblings and stepmother(s). In my opinion, God is sharing these stories to show us that we will see parents who may have more than one wife or husband with several kids from different parents. And other races, ethnicity, background, and religious beliefs should not matter. We should get to know our stepsiblings and support and lift them—this type of situation we see happening in our families. Stepsibling fights and being hostile with one another will not get you anywhere. We must love one another unconditionally.

Shahira Amin, a freelance journalist based in Cairo, Egypt, explained that the Jews are descendants of Abraham's son Isaac, and the Arabs are descendants of Ishmael. Ishmael was a servant's son (Genesis 16:1–16), and Isaac was the son who inherited the promised land that God promised to Abraham (Genesis 21:1–3). In Genesis 16:11–12, an angel prophesied that Ishmael "will live far away from his relatives and he will be like a wild donkey, fighting everyone and everyone fighting him." I think this is a sin consequence that Abraham and Sarah brought about on themselves. Sarah could not wait until God blessed her with a son. She decided to think on her own without praying and asking God first. She told Abraham to marry Hagar, her servant, and they had a son named Ishmael.

Isaac Married Rebekah

Abraham's son Isaac was forty years old when he married Rebekah, the daughter of Bethuel and sister of Laban. The Aramean was from northern Syria (Genesis 25:19–20, Deuteronomy 26:5) and descendants of Shem (Genesis 10).

Twenty years later, Rebekah and Isaac still had no children. Like his father, Abraham prayed and asked God to let his wife have a child. The Lord answered and blessed her with twins (Genesis 25:21, Romans 9:10–13).

Esau and Jacob Were Born

Rebekah knew that she would have twins because she felt them kicking and fighting in her stomach. "She thought, 'Why is this happening to me?' and asked God, 'Why are the twins fighting'" (Genesis 25:22)? The Lord answered, "Your two sons will become two separate nations. The younger of the two will be stronger, and the older son will be his servant" (Genesis 25:23). Rebekah's faith was strong. Whenever she had a question about her life, she prayed. Where is your faith in God? Are you in prayer with our Lord? Are you living by faith and trusting God?

When Rebekah delivered her sons, the first one came out red. His skin and hair color was red and hairy, so he was named Esau, which means red. The second one came out holding on to his brother's heel, so they named him Jacob, which means "holder of the heel." Isaac was sixty years old when they were born (Genesis 25:24–26, Hosea 12:3). Esau's tribe was the Edomites. There is no mention of Jacob belonging to one specific tribe. Although his name changed to Israel (Genesis 32:28). I think he identified himself with the Israelites.

Esau Sells His Birthrights

Esau, the oldest brother, sold his birthright to his younger brother, Jacob. Birthright means the oldest child in a family usually is in charge after the parents die or inherit more than the other siblings. But in this case, Esau was not worried about being the oldest or getting the blessings the oldest child would inherit.

As the brothers grew older, Esau was a man that liked the outdoors. He enjoyed hunting with his father, Isaac. Esau was the hunter who liked playing wild games outdoors, whereas his brother Jacob liked staying home in the tent with his mother Rebekah (Genesis 25:27, Hosea 12:3). He was known as the shepherd. It was evident that Rebekah favored and loved Jacob more because he stayed in the tent with her. Isaac was close to his son Esau because they hunted and killed wild animals. He would bring home meat from the wild animals, which pleased his father (Genesis 25:28), but Jacob was Rebekah's favorite one.

One day, Jacob was cooking some stew when Esau came home hungry and said, "I am starving to death! Give me some of that red stew right now!" That is how he got his tribe's name Edomites (Genesis 25:29–30).

Jacob replied, "Sell me your rights as the firstborn son" (Genesis 25:31, Deuteronomy 21:16–17). Esau was so hungry he was not thinking and answered his brother, "I am about to die, what good will those rights do me" (Genesis 25:32, Mark 8:36).

Jacob said, "Promise me your birthrights, here and now!" And that is what Esau did (Genesis 25:33). Jacob immediately gave his brother Esau some bread bean stew. And when Esau finished eating and drinking, he got up and walked away, showing no regard for his firstborn rights (Genesis 25:34). Esau was an emotional person who did not think about the consequences of giving up his birthrights. Until the next time. I love you!

Love,
Grandma

Twenty-Sixth Chapter Letter

Isaac Meets King Abimelech

Greetings, my grandkids. I hope all is well with you. Today is Monday, April 12, 2021. It has been seventy-one days living with Grandma Josie. I miss my home and husband, but we see each other several days out of the week. However, I feel blessed to care for my mom 24/7 and write and study God's word.

In Genesis, chapter 26, I will be writing about Isaac and how he met Abimelech. I will share about his son Esau marrying two foreign women. I talk about the famine during Isaac's time in this chapter. A famine is when there is a shortage of food. In this chapter, God reestablished the covenant/promises with Isaac, the same one he made with his father, Abraham. You will notice parallels to Abraham's life in this letter.

Isaac was living near Beer-lahai-roi, where his sons were born. He was forced to move to Gerar because the field was not producing grain, but Isaac asked Abimelech of the Philistines for grain (Genesis 26:1). The Lord had appeared to Isaac and said, "Isaac, stay away from Egypt! I will show you where I want you to go." When Abraham ran out of food, he moved to Egypt (Genesis 12:10–11). God did not want Isaac to go to Egypt because they were worshiping idols. God told Isaac, "You will live in Gerar as a foreigner, but I will be with you and bless you. I will keep my promise to your father Abraham by giving this land to you and your descendants" (Genesis 26:2–3, Hebrews 11:9). Thus, God's covenant (pledge) was made to Isaac.

The Lord told Isaac that he will have many descendants as there are stars in the sky and that they would get this land (Gerar). God said, "They will be a blessing to every nation on earth because Abraham did everything the Lord told him to do (Genesis 26:4–5). What a gift to Isaac! Because his father was a faithful man to our Lord, Isaac is receiving the benefits. Blessing can be handed down to the next generations as well as consequences for doing sinful things. What you do today will affect your life in the future and your kid's life.

Isaac moved to Gerar with his beautiful wife, Rebekah. She was so beautiful he thought someone might kill him to take her, so he told everyone in Gerar that Rebekah was his sister (Genesis 26:6–7). Remember his father Abraham did the same thing with his wife Sarah when he went to Gerar. He told the people that Sarah was his sister because he thought someone might take her (Genesis 20:2). Do you see the parallel? They both lied and did not have to. They should have trusted God to see them through their fears. It is not good to lie. Try your best to be honest, even if you think it may hurt you or others.

After Isaac lived in Gerar for a while, Abimelech happened to look out of a window and saw Isaac hugging and kissing his wife Rebekah (Genesis 26:8). Abimelech called Isaac in to see him. "Rebekah must be your wife! Why did you say she was your sister" (Genesis 26:9)? The king was so upset and afraid. He said to Isaac, "Don't you know what you have done?" Abimelech shouted. "If someone had slept with Rebekah, you would have made our whole nation guilty" (Genesis 26:10, Exodus 32:21)! Abimelech warned his people that anyone who even touches Isaac or Rebekah would be put to death (Genesis 26:11).

God spoke to Abimelech in a dream before regarding Abraham and Sarah. God said, "You have taken a married woman, and for this, you will die" (Genesis 20:3)! Abimelech knew from past experiences that Abraham's God is real, and he would receive consequences. Therefore, he was so mad at Isaac for not being honest.

Isaac planted grain and had a good harvest that same year. The Lord had blessed him, and he became phenomenally successful and wealthy (Genesis 26:12–13, Job 42:12, Matthew 13:8, Proverbs 10:22). The Philistines were jealous of Isaac's blessings because of the many sheep, goats, and servants he owned. Abimelech's men clogged up the water wells that Abraham's servants had dug up before his death (Genesis 26:14–15). Abimelech's men envied Isaac and asked him to leave his country because he had become too powerful to stay there (Genesis 26:16, Exodus 1:9). It was wrong and hateful for Abimelech's men to clog up the wells. All they did was bring karma to themselves.

Being envious of someone's success is not wise. Instead, be proud and happy for your friends or relatives for becoming successful. Isaac received the blessing from God, and all good comes from God! Isaac's servants dug another well, and the shepherds again argued with Isaac's servants. So that well was named "Jealous" (Genesis 26:21). Isaac's servant finally dug one more well, but there was no arguing this time, and the well was named "Lots of Room" because the Lord had given them room and made them successful (Genesis 26:22). It was Isaac's season to be blessed.

We will all have seasons in our lives like Isaac. Isaac did not get mad at Abimelech's men for clogging the wells. He refused to fight with them. He turned the cheek and ended up receiving more blessings from God. It is not good to do evil with evil. Try to be the bigger person when someone tries to hurt you. You will be blessed. God said, "Let me handle the consequences." It is not our job. Evil people are emotionally broken and have personal problems you cannot fix. It is their problem, not yours! They have to want to help themselves first.

Isaac moved on to Beersheba, which is west of Gerar. The Lord appeared to Isaac at night and told him, "Do not be afraid! I am the God who was worshiped by your father, Abraham, who was my servant. I will be with you and bless you, and because of Abraham, I will give you many descendants" (Genesis 26:23–24). Isaac, like his father Abraham, built an altar there and worshiped the Lord. Here again, Isaac followed his father Abraham's example by building an altar to the Lord so he can worship God (Genesis 26:25). What are you doing to honor and thank God for your blessings? I built the temple in my yard to worship and thank God for my blessings.

Abimelech Made Peace with Isaac

Meantime, Abimelech left Gerar with his advisor Ahuzzath and his army commander Phicol to see Isaac (Genesis 26:26). Isaac was surprised to see Abimelech and his men. When Isaac saw them coming his way, Isaac asked, "What are you doing here? You sent me away because you hated me?" (Genesis 26:27). Abimelech replied, "We know for sure the Lord is with you, so we have decided there should be a peace treaty between us. So let us make a solemn agreement not to harm each other." Abimelech continued by saying, "Remember, we had never hurt you when we sent you away, we let you go in peace" (Genesis 26:28–29).

They saw how the Lord had blessed Isaac and were worried. Finally, Abimelech said, "The Lord has truly blessed you" (Genesis 26:29). It is truly a blessing when others can see your gifts from God. Recall Abraham experiencing the same thing with Abimelech in chapter 21. He and his men were afraid of God; instead of knowing God, they ran away to avoid asking about him.

Isaac was a humble person who held a big feast for them. He did not want drama. Isaac acknowledged the separation was peaceful but knew they were envious of his success. Abimelech was worried because he did not want God to punish him for treating Isaac mean. They all ate and drank. The next day, Isaac and the others made a solemn agreement, then everyone went on their way peacefully (Genesis 26:30–31). Later that day, Isaac's men came to him and said, "We have struck water!" Again! So "Isaac named the well Shibah, and the town is still called Beersheba today" (Genesis 26:32).

Esau Marries his Foreign Wives

Esau was forty years old when he married Judith, the daughter of Beeri the Hittite, and Basemath, the daughter of Elon the Hittite. These two women brought many heartaches to Esau's parents, Isaac and Rebekah (Genesis 26:34–35) because they were nonbelievers. Esau was an impulsive and emotional man. In the following letter, I will talk more about his behavior.

The Hittite tribe comes from Ham, the son of Noah. Remember, we all come from one of Noah's three sons—Shem, Ham, and Japheth (Genesis 10). It is getting late, and I will be getting ready for bed. Until the next time! God bless you.

Love,
Grandma

Twenty-Seventh Chapter Letter

Isaac Gives Jacob His Blessings

Hello, my beautiful grandkids. I hope all is well. Today is Tuesday, April 13, 2021. I am still here at Grandma Josie's house, caring for her. I feel so blessed that God has allowed me to be here to care for her and write this book. He is an awesome God!

In this letter, I will write about what happened in Genesis, chapter 27, how Isaac gave Jacob his blessings, and Rebekah played a trick on her husband and lied to her sons. She favored Jacob, and Esau felt betrayed by his family. This story centers around family separation caused by the parents. She let the devil win, and it destroyed her family.

Isaac was getting old, and he knew he was going blind, so he called out to his first son, Esau, who answered, "Father, what can I do for you" (Genesis 27:1). Isaac said, "I am old and might die at any time. So, take your bow and arrows and go out to the fields and kill a wild animal and cook some of that tasty food that I love so much and bring it to me. I want to eat it one more time and give you my blessings before I die" (Genesis 27:3–4, Proverbs 27:1).

Rebekah was nearby listening to the request made by her husband, and as soon as Esau ran out to go hunting, she immediately pulled her other son, Jacob, aside and told him what she had overheard (Genesis 27:5). She told Jacob, "I heard your father tell Esau to kill a wild animal and cook some tasty food before he dies. Your father wants to bless your brother with the Lord as his witness" (Genesis 27:6–7).

Rebekah was wrong! She was dishonest and teaching her son that it was okay to lie. Her mistake was favoring one son over another. Her husband Isaac does not know what is going on because he was going blind. There will be consequences that will follow Rebekah. The family will be separated. But God knew this beforehand.

Rebekah told Jacob, "Now, son, listen carefully to what I want you to do. Go kill two of your best young goats and bring them to me. I will cook the tasty food your father loves so much" (Genesis 27:8–9). Rebekah wanted her favorite son Jacob to receive the blessings. She told Jacob to go take the food to his dad so "he can eat it and give you the blessings before he dies (Genesis 27:10). But Jacob said, "My brother Esau is a hairy man, remember, and I am not" (Genesis 27:11). Rebekah took things into her own hands instead of allowing God to do his work. God told her while she was pregnant, back in Genesis 25:23, that her sons will be two separate nations and that the younger would serve the older son by being his servant. God had already planned this, but she did it her way. Grandkids, listen to the Holy Spirit that lives in you or your gut feelings when you are thinking about betraying the love of your life. It is not worth it in the long run.

Jacob was worried that his dad, Isaac, would know who he was because he was not hairy. Jacob said, "If my father touches me and realizes I am trying to trick him, he will put a curse on me instead of giving me blessings" (Genesis 27:12, Deuteronomy 27:18). Rebekah demanded that Jacob do what she had requested. She said, "Let his curse fall on me! Just do what I am asking you to do and bring me the goat meat" (Genesis 27:13, Matthew 27:25). Jacob brought her the meat, and she cooked the tasty food that Isaac liked. Rebekah then took her son Esau's best clothes and put them on Jacob (Genesis 27:14–15, Proverbs 23:3). She covered the smooth part of his hands and neck with goatskin and gave him bread and the food she cooked. Jacob was nervous while he was approaching his dad. He said, "Father, here I am. I am Esau, your firstborn, and I have done what you have requested. Can you please sit up and eat the meat I have made for you, and then you can give me your blessings" (Genesis 27:16–19)?

Isaac could not believe that Esau killed an animal that fast and asked him, "Son, how did you find the animal so quickly?" Jacob lied and said, "The Lord was kind to me and helped find the animal" (Genesis 27:20). Jacob was not sure who Esau was, so he asked him to come close to touch him.

Isaac said, "My son, come closer, where I can feel you and make sure you are my son Esau." Jacob went close to his dad, and Isaac touched Jacob. "You sound like Jacob, but feels like Esau." Isaac blessed Jacob thinking he was Esau. Isaac asked him, "Are you sure you are my son Esau?"

Jacob answered, "Yes, I am."

Isaac said, "Okay, serve me the wild meat, and I will give you my blessings." Jacob gave him some of the food he requested, and he ate it. He also gave him some wine, and he drank it (Genesis 27:21–25).

Isaac said, "Son, come over here and kiss me," and Jacob kissed him. Isaac said, "You smell like my son Esau, like the wild field, and the Lord has blessed you" (Genesis 27:26–27). Isaac believed he was talking to his son Esau but giving his blessing to Jacob. "God will bless you, my son, with dew from heaven and with fertile fields, rich with grain and grapes. Nations will be your servants and bow down to you" (Genesis 27:28, Deuteronomy 33:28, Hebrews 11:20). Isaac continued by saying he would rule over his brothers and that they will kneel at his feet. And that if anyone cursed him, they would be cursed, and if anyone blessed him, they would be blessed (Genesis 27:29, Zephaniah 2:8).

As soon as Isaac gave Jacob his blessing, he left home, and his brother Esau came back from hunting. Esau cooked the tasty food his father asked him to do and brought it to him. He was so excited and happy to be able to feed his dad. He said, "Father, please sit up and eat the meat I have brought you so that you can give me your blessings" (Genesis 27:30–31).

Isaac asked, "Who are you?"

"I am Esau, your first son" (Genesis 27:32, Exodus 13:2).

Isaac started trembling and did not understand. Finally, he said, "Then who brought me some wild meat right before you came in? I ate it and gave him a blessing that cannot be taken back" (Genesis 27:33).

Esau cried out loud and begged his father to bless him, but it was too late. Esau cried, saying, "Father, give me a blessing!"

His father said, "Your brother tricked me and must have stolen your blessings" (Genesis 27:34–35).

Esau was so mad at his brother Jacob. He said, "My brother deserves the name Jacob because he already cheated me twice. The first time he cheated me out of my rights as the firstborn son, and now he has cheated me out of my blessings." Esau asked his father, "Don't you have any blessings left for me?" (Genesis 27:36).

The name Jacob in Hebrew is "Cheat." That was why Esau said his brother Jacob deserves that name. This situation must have been difficult for their mother to witness. She was probably hurting inside to overhear her son cry out loud like a baby and beg his father; it was a sad day for them. Everyone was emotionally injured in the process. This type of pain will stay in your memory for a lifetime. It is best not to put yourself in this type of situation. Treat your children equally and always communicate with your children and state why you may treat one child differently than the other.

Isaac felt horrible for his son Esau. So he said, "My son, I have made Jacob the ruler over you and your brothers, and all of you will be his servants. I have promised him all the grains and grapes that he needs. There is nothing left for you" (Genesis 27:37, 2 Samuel 8:14).

Esau answered by saying, "Don't you have more than one blessing? You can give me a blessing too" (Genesis 27:38, Hebrews 12:17). He then began to cry out loud again.

Isaac said to Esau, "Your home will be far from that fertile land, where dew comes down from the heavens. You will live by the power of your sword and by your brother's servants. But when you decide to be free, you will break loose" (Genesis 27:39, Hebrews 11:20).

Esau hated his brother Jacob because of what he did, stealing his blessings. So he said when his father, Isaac, would die, he would kill his brother Jacob. Of course, his mother, Rebekah, found out what he was planning to do and went to tell Jacob what Esau was plotting.

Rebekah said to Jacob, "Son, your brother Esau is waiting for a time to kill you. Now listen carefully and do what I say. Go to my brother Laban's home in Haran and stay with him for a while until your brother stops being angry and forgets about what you did to him. Then, I will send for you to come home. Why should I lose both of you" (Genesis 27:40–45, 2 Samuel 8:14, 2 Kings 8:20, Psalm 64:5).

As you can see, Rebekah was not taking any responsibility for what she had done to separate her family. She lied and manipulated, and in turn, her family suffered. Remember when Rebekah was pregnant and her sons were fighting in her stomach and God told her that her sons would be fighting each other, but God did not ask Rebekah to help him do his work. God told her the two would have their nations. He had a plan, but she took it upon herself to do things her way. Rebekah taught Jacob to lie and cheat. Esau could not believe his family turned on him. He felt betrayed. Have you ever felt like Esau? If so, how did you handle your situation? Esau overcame his pain and suffering in the future. God blessed him and his family. Jacob was a good man but learned to lie.

Rebekah later complained to her husband, Isaac, saying, "Those Hittite wives of Esau are making my life miserable! If Jacob marries a Hittite woman, I would be better off dead" (Genesis 27:46). These women were ungodly. Rebekah was a woman who loved her family but showed favoritism between her sons which caused the separation between the family. She lost in the end because her sons were becoming enemies. Until the next time.

Love,
Grandma

Twenty-Eighth Chapter Letter

Isaac's Instructions to Jacob

Good morning to my beautiful grandkids. Today is Saturday, April 24, 2021, and it has been eighty-three days living with Grandma Josie. She has her good days and her bad days. Her mind continues to decline right in from of my eyes. I know God is in control of her life. The coronavirus continues to be a problem in our world. However, this month, many schools and other businesses have opened and are back in business.

I will be writing to you about what happened in Genesis, chapter 28, which is a continuation of the last letter. Rebekah was allowing the devil to separate her family. Isaac, Jacob's father, called him to give him his blessings and inform him to marry a woman from their tribe. He instructed him not to marry a woman from the Canaanite tribe. I will share how Esau married another woman and about Jacob's dream.

Isaac said, "Jacob, don't marry any of those Canaanite women. Go at once to your mother's father, Bethuel, in northern Syria and choose a wife from one of Uncle Laban, your mother's brother" (Genesis 28:1–2, Hosea 2:12). Isaac prayed for Jacob. "I pray that God All-Powerful will bless you with many descendants and let you become a great nation. May God bless you with the land he gave Abraham so that you will take over this land where we now live as foreigners" (Genesis 28:3–5). Isaac then sent Jacob to live with Rebekah's brother Laban, the son of Bethuel the Aramean (Genesis

28:6). Recall in chapter letter 24, Abraham sent his servant to find his son Isaac a wife from his hometown? And Rebekah was the woman to be Isaac's wife. That is where Isaac and Rebekah were sending Jacob, to the same town.

Esau Marries Ishmael's Daughter

Esau, at this point, was hurt because his parents sent his brother Jacob away. He also found out that his father Isaac had blessed Jacob and warned him not to marry a Canaanite woman. Esau knew that his parents sent his brother to find a wife in northern Syria and how Jacob obeyed (Genesis 28:7). He already had several wives, but he knew that his parents hated the Canaanite women. So he wanted to try to please his parents and "married Ishmael's daughter Mahalath, who was the sister of Nebaioth and granddaughter of Abraham" (Genesis 28:8–9), all in the family.

Recall Ishmael is Isaac's stepbrother, same father, Abraham, but different mother. Ishmael's mother was Sarah's Egyptian servant. Everyone is related in this story. The families are separated because of parents having a favorite son, dishonesty among family members, and wanting to do things their way without praying about their situation, the same problem in families today. The devil wins when family members are angry at each other. The decisions and choices you make today affect what happens in the future. Be careful and pray before you make any dishonest decisions when it comes to family. Ask God to help you!

Jacob's Dream at Bethel

Jacob left the town and headed toward Beersheba and started for Haran. "At sunset, he stopped for the night and went to sleep, resting his head on a large rock. In a dream, he saw a ladder that reached from earth to heaven, and God's angels were going up and down on it" (Genesis 28:10–12, Acts 7:2). God was standing by the ladder and said, "I am the Lord God whom Abraham and Isaac worshiped," his grandfather and father. God told him that he would give him and his family the land he was sleeping in (Genesis 28:13). God said to Jacob that his descendants would spread all around the earth in all directions, and they will become numerous as the specks on dust. "Your family will be a blessing to all people" (Genesis 28:14).

God said to Jacob in his dream, "Where you are, I will watch over you, and then later I will bring you back to this land. I will never leave you. I will do all I have promised" (Genesis 28:15). Jacob woke up instantly and thought to himself, "'The Lord is in this place, and I did not know it.' Jacob was afraid and said, 'This is a fearsome place! It must be the house of God and the ladder to heaven'" (Genesis 28:16–17, Exodus 3:5, Joshua 5:15, Psalm 68:35). Jacob never had an encounter with God; this was the first time, in his dream. He believed in God because he witnessed his father, Isaac, having a relationship with God.

The following morning, Jacob got up early and took the rock he used to dedicate to God. Jacob named the place Bethel before it was called Luz (Genesis 28:18–19). Jacob started negotiating with God. He promised God, "If you go with me and watch over me as I travel, and if you give me food and clothes and bring me safely home again, you will be my God. And this rock will be your home, and I will give you a tenth of everything you give me" (Genesis 28:20–22, Leviticus 27:30, Judges11:30–31).

Jacob was at the beginning stages of getting to know God, so I think he felt comfortable speaking to him in that matter. Going back home was not in God's plan for him. God had other plans for his future. He was headed for a lifelong journey. Giving 10 percent to God was Jacob's way of thanking him for having his back. It is getting late, 10:50 p.m. And I thank God I was able to finish this letter today. Until next time.

Love,
Grandma

Twenty-Ninth Chapter Letter

Jacob Arrives at Laban's House

Greetings, grandkids. I hope all is well. It is 6:40 p.m., Monday, April 26, 2021. Today is eighty-five days living with Grandma Josie. This morning, I went out with Nina, a friend, and had breakfast, and shortly after, Grandma Josie and I went out to get a manicure and pedicure. So it was a good day.

I will be writing to you about what happened in Genesis, chapter 29. In the last letter, I wrote about Jacob getting sent away because his brother, Esau, was angry at him for stealing his blessings. The story continues with Jacob's parents sending him to his uncle's house in Haran. In this letter, I will write about Jacob falling in love with his cousin Rachel and how his uncle tricked him into marrying his older daughter, Leah, first. The story of Jacob gets more interesting as he was away from his home and learned to lean on God for direction.

As Jacob traveled to the east, he looked out in the field and saw a well where shepherds took their sheep for water (Genesis 29:1–2, Numbers 23:7). The shepherds would roll the stone away when all their sheep had gathered there. Then after the sheep had been watered, the shepherds would roll the rock back over the mouth of the well (Genesis 29:3).

> Jacob asked the shepherds, "Where are you from?" They said, "We are from Haran." Then, Jacob asked, "Do you know Nahor's grand-

son Laban?" "Yes, we do," they replied. "How is he?" Jacob asked. They said, "He is fine, and here comes his daughter Rachel with the sheep" (Genesis 29:3–6, Exodus 2:16).

Jacob told the shepherds, "Look, the sun is still high up in the sky, and it is early to bring in the rest of the flocks, water your sheep and take them back in the pasture." The shepherds said, "We cannot do that until they all get here, and the rock has been rolled away from the well." (Genesis 29:7–8)

While Jacob talked to the shepherds, he saw his cousin Rachel come up with her father's sheep, rolled the rock away, and watered the sheep (Genesis 29:9–10). Jacob immediately held Rachel in his arms and kissed her, and started crying because he was happy. He told Rachel he was the son of her aunt Rebekah, and she ran home to tell her father about Jacob (Genesis 29:11–12).

After Rachel told her dad, Laban, he ran out to meet Jacob. Laban hugged and kissed Jacob and brought him to his home. Jacob told his uncle what happened at his home with his brother Esau and how his mother told him to come to Haran. Laban said, "You are my nephew, and you are like one of my own family" (Genesis 29:13–14, Judges 9:2). Jacob was happy to be among family members. Remember Jacob was a mama's boy who liked to stay in the tent with his mother.

Jacob Marries Leah and Rachel

For one month, Jacob lived with his uncle when Laban said, "You should not work without pay just because you are a relative of mine." Laban asked Jacob, "What would you like me to pay you" (Genesis 29:15)? Laban had two daughters, Leah and Rachel. Leah was older than Rachel, but her eyes did not sparkle, while Rachel was beautiful and had a great shape. Jacob fell in love with Rachel as soon as he saw her. Jacob told his uncle, "If you let me marry Rachel, I will work for you for seven years" (Genesis 29:16–18).

Jacob's uncle said, "I should let you marry her than for someone else to have her, so stay and work for me." Jacob worked hard for seven years, but the time seemed like only days because he loved Rachel (Genesis 29:19–20). When the seven years were up, he told his uncle, "The time is here, and I want to marry Rachel now!" Laban planned a big feast and invited all their neighbors (Genesis 29:21–22, Judges 15:1). That evening, Uncle Laban brought his older daughter Leah to Jacob, who married her and spent the night with him. The uncle gave Leah a servant woman named Zilpah (Genesis 29:23–24). The following morning, Jacob realized that he was married to Leah and asked his uncle, "Why did you do this to me? I worked to get Rachel. Why did you trick me?" His uncle said, "In our country, the older daughter must get married first." So Laban told Jacob, "After you spend this week with your wife Leah, you may marry her sister Rachel after you work another seven years for me" (Genesis 29:25–27, 1 Samuel 28:12).

Do you see how Jacob's Uncle Laban lied and tricked him into marrying Leah instead of Rachel? Remember Jacob cheated his brother out of his birthright and lied to his dad by saying he was Esau to get the blessings. When you lie and cheat people, it will always come back around ten times harder. Jacob worked an extra seven years to get the woman he loved. You must always pray and think before deciding to be dishonest to others because you will get your karma tenfold. It is a sin!

At the end of the celebration, Uncle Laban allowed Jacob to marry Rachel and gave her his servant, Bilhah. Jacob loved Rachel more than he did her sister, Leah (Genesis 29:28–30). Uncle Laban was a greedy family member who used Jacob. Jacob wanted Rachel so bad he did whatever it took to get her. Jacob was a humble man trying to survive, and his uncle took advantage of him. He worked fourteen years for his two wives and an additional two years to make his uncle happy. The agreement between Uncle Laban and Jacob was for him to work seven years for Rachel, which he was tricked into and ended up with Leah. So he worked another seven for Rachel.

That was their agreement. But Jacob served an extra seven years until he decided to move on with his family. There are people in the world who will take your kindness for weakness. And you may have greedy family members who will take advantage of you. Do not allow it!

The Lord knew Jacob loved Rachel more than Leah, so he blessed Leah with children and not Rachel (Genesis 29:31, Psalm 127:3). First, Leah gave birth to a son named Reuben because she said, "The Lord has taken away her sorrow." Then she said, "Now, my husband will love me more than Rachel." Next, she had a second son named Simeon because she said, "The Lord has heard that my husband does not love me." Then Leah had a third son. When the third son was born, she said, "Now my husband will hold me close." So she named him Levi. Finally, Leah had one more son and named him Judah because she said, "I will praise the Lord" (Genesis 29:32–35, Exodus 4:31, Deuteronomy 26:7, 1 Samuel 2:3, Matthew 1:2).

The Lord blessed Leah with four sons, and this is the beginning of the twelve tribes—Reuben, Simeon, Levi, and Judah. They will have their land and tribe names and their language. Rachel and Jacob must wait on God's timing to be blessed with a baby. Remember, Abraham and Sarah had to wait for God to bless them with Isaac. Sarah refused to wait on God's timing, so she had her Egyptian servant marry Abraham, and they had Ishmael. God has his plan for each one of you. But it is on his time, not yours. Stay in prayer. God does answer prayers on his time. Until the next time. Good night.

Love,
Grandma

Thirtieth Chapter Letter

Problems between the Sisters, Leah and Rachel

Greetings, my beloved grandkids. I hope you are well and walking in love with your brothers and sisters. Today is Monday, April 26, 2021. In the last chapter, Jacob traveled to his uncle Laban's house, lived there, married two of his cousins, and had four sons with his wife Leah. In Genesis, chapter 30, I will share how the sisters Leah and Rachel are jealous of each other. Jacob married his wives' servants and had more sons. The twelve tribes are slowly forming. Toward the end of this chapter, God finally answered Rachel's prayer and blessed her with a son named Joseph.

Rachel was so angry and jealous of her sister, Leah, for having children. She told Jacob, "I will die if you do not give me children." Jacob got upset and said, "Do not get mad and blame me! I'm not God" (Genesis 30:1–2). Rachel was so hurt and jealous she said to Jacob, "Here, take my servant Bilhah, have children with her. Let the baby be born on my knees to show that they are mine" (Genesis 30:3, Job 3:2).

Remember, her grandmother Sarah did the same thing with her servant Hagar. Do you see the same patterns in families with men and women? Men are obeying their wives in terms of marrying and having children with their servants. The women were not patient and want to do things their way instead of waiting on God. The devil seemed to be influencing these women instead of them choosing to be patient.

Rachel let her husband marry her servant Bilhah, and they had a son. Rachel named him Dan because she said, "God had answered my prayers. He has judged and given me a son" (Genesis 30:4–6, Lamentations 3:59). Bilhah and Jacob had a second son, and Rachel was so happy. She said, "I have struggled hard with my sister, but now I have won." So Rachel named the boy Naphtali" (Genesis 30:7–8). Leah saw her sister Rachel's servant having children and tried having more but realized she could not at that moment, so she let Jacob marry her servant Zilpah and she had a son, and Leah named him Gad (Genesis 30:9–10). Leah felt lucky and said, "I am happy now, and all the women can see how pleased I am." Leah's servant had another son and named him Asher (Genesis 30:11–13, Luke 1:48). The two sisters prayed and asked God to give them a child, but it appeared that God only answered Leah's prayers and not Rachel's. God is in control, and when he wants to bless women with children, he will in his time. The two sisters competed to see who can have more children than the other. It seems like they both wanted to make Jacob happy, but he loved Rachel more.

Love Flowers

It was wheat harvest season, and Reuben saw some love flowers and took them to his mother, Leah. Rachel was nearby and wanted some and asked her sister Leah if she could have some beautiful flowers. Leah said, "It is bad enough you stole my husband! Now you want my son's love flowers." Rachel replied, "All right, let me have some love flowers, and you can sleep with Jacob tonight" (Genesis 30:14–15). The two sisters were constantly in battle with each other trying to win Jacob's love.

Later that evening, when Jacob came home from working in the fields, Leah told him, "You're sleeping with me tonight. I hired you with my son's love flowers." They slept together that night (Genesis 30:16), and God answered Leah's prayer by blessing her with a fifth son. Leah shouted, "God has rewarded me for letting Jacob marry my servant, and she named her son Issachar" (Genesis 30:17–18). Leah was so surprised and thrilled God had given her a sixth son, and she named him Zebulun. She later had a daughter and called her Dinah (Genesis 30:19–21).

God finally answered Rachel's prayer and blessed her with a son. Rachel said, "God has taken away my disgrace, I will name my boy Joseph, and I will pray that the Lord bless me with another son" (Genesis 30:22–24, Luke 1:25). As mentioned before, God will answer prayers in his time. We must have patience.

Jacob Leaves Uncle Laban's Home

Shortly after Joseph was born, Jacob said to Uncle Laban, "Release me from our agreement and let me go to my home country. You know I worked hard for you, so let me take my wives and children and leave" (Genesis 30:25–26, Hosea 12:12).

Laban replied, "If you are my friend, stay on, and I will pay whatever you ask. I know God blessed me because of you" (Genesis 30:27–28, 1 Timothy 5:8).

Jacob said, "I do not want you to pay me anything. Just do me one favor, and I will take care of your sheep and goats. Let me go through your flock and herds and take the sheep and goats spotted or speckled and the black lambs. That is all I need from you" (Genesis 30:29–32, 1 Timothy 5:8). Jacob told his uncle, "In the future, you can easily find out if I've been honest. Look and see if any my animals are either spotted or speckled, or if the lambs are black. If they are not, they have been stolen from you" (Genesis 30:33, Psalm 37:6).

Uncle Laban said, "Okay, I agree to that" (Genesis 30:34).

Before the end of the day, Laban separated his spotted and speckled animals and the black lambs from the others (Genesis 30:35). He had his sons watch over the animals. Uncle Laban made Jacob keep the rest of the sheep and goats at a distance of three days (Genesis 30:36). It took his sons three days to reach Jacob. Jacob kept his promise and cared for the flock, and while he was out in the field, he cut branches from some poplar trees, some almonds, and evergreen trees. He peeled off some bark and made the branches look spotted and speckled (Genesis 30:37). Jacob put the branches where the sheep and goats can see while drinking from the water trough. A trough is a long open container animal eats and drinks out of. "The goats mated there in front of the branches, and their young were spotted and speckled" (Genesis 30:38–39).

Jacob Built His Wealth

The sheep that were Jacob's uncle's were already spotted. And when the others were ready to mate near the drinking place, Jacob made sure they were facing the direction of the spotted and black ones. In this way, Jacob built up his flock of sheep for himself and did not put them with his uncle Laban's flock (Genesis 30:40).

When the stronger sheep were mating near the drinking place, Jacob made sure that the spotted branches were there. However, he did not put out the branches when the weaker animals were mating. Instead, Jacob made sure he got all the healthy animals, and his uncle got the weaker ones (Genesis 30:41–42). As a result, Jacob soon became wealthy and successful. He owned many sheep, goats, camels, donkeys, and a lot of servants (Genesis 30:43). Until the next time.

Love,
Grandma

Thirty-First Chapter Letter

Jacob Runs from Uncle Laban's Home

Hi, grandkids. I hope all is well. Today is May 2, 2021, 7:30 p.m. I have been living with Grandma Josie for ninety-one days. I continue to have good and bad days with her. It is sad to see her not remember what she does every minute of the day. God bless her!

Genesis, chapter 31, is a continuation of the last letter. Jacob finally parted with his Uncle Laban's home after twenty years of his uncle using him. This chapter will share how Laban and his sons were mad at Jacob because they knew he was rich and had many goods. Finally, God spoke to Jacob and told him to go back to where he was born in Canaan.

Uncle Laban met up with Jacob to find out if he had stolen an idol from his home, but before he met up with him, God warned Laban in a dream not to say a word to Jacob, or there will be consequences. By the end of the chapter, Laban and Jacob agreed to make peace. This chapter is exceptionally long. It has fifty-five verses, but the story gets interesting because Jacob was on his own, trusting God to hold his hand one step at a time. He learned to walk by faith!

Jacob heard through his associates that his cousins were complaining that he was doing well and thriving. Jacob was wealthy, and his cousins felt their father helped him become rich, which is false (Genesis 31:1, Psalm 49:16). Jacob also noticed that his uncle Laban and extended family members were not as friendly to him as before (Genesis 31:2), and God knew they were not warm toward him anymore. So the Lord told Jacob to "go back to your relatives in the land of your ancestors, and I will bless you" (Genesis 31:3).

It is sad when your cousins or uncles and extended family members are jealous of your success in life. But unfortunately, trouble starts in our home environment with our families and extended family. But you can be the bigger person and treat your family the way Jesus would, with love. We all have family problems, but they can be resolved by staying in prayer and asking God to help with the family issues.

Jacob Sent for Leah and Rachel

Jacob asked one of his servants to give his two wives a message. Jacob wanted his wives to meet him in the field where he kept his sheep (Genesis 31:4). Jacob told them that their father was not friendly toward him like before. He said, "But the God my ancestors worshiped has been on my side" (Genesis 31:5). Jacob told Leah and Rachel, "You know I have worked hard for your father, even though he cheated me by changing my wages ten times." But God had Jacob's back the entire time (Genesis 31:6–7, Numbers 14:22). God was not going to allow Uncle Laban to hurt Jacob.

Jacob told his wives, "When your father said the speckled sheep would be my wages, and all of them were speckled, then he would change his mind and say the spotted ones would be mine, and all of them were spotted" (Genesis 31:8). So Uncle Laban manipulated Jacob, and because of that, God took the sheep and goats (Genesis 31:9).

Jacob told his wives, "Once when the flocks were mating, I dreamed that all the rams were either spotted or speckled" (Genesis 31:10). "Then God's angel called me by my name, and I answered, and He said, 'Notice that all the rams are either spotted or speckled, and I know everything Laban was doing to you'" (Genesis 31:11–12, Exodus 3:7).

God said, "I am the God you worshiped at Bethel when you poured olive oil on a rock and made a promise to me. Leave here right away and return to the land where you were born" (Genesis 31:13).

Uncle Laban was not satisfied with Jacob's hard work all those years. He was not content with what he had, and he wanted more. God tells us not to fall in love with money and materials but to be satisfied with what we have. The Lord said he would never leave us or forsake us (Hebrews 13:5). So everything ended up backfiring on Uncle Laban, and it will with people who try to cheat others out of what they have earned.

Rachel and Leah tell Jacob, "There is nothing left for us to inherit from our father. He has even treated us like foreigners and cheated us out of the bride price that should have been ours" (Genesis 31:14–15). So Rachel and Leah told Jacob to do whatever God told him to do because the property God took from their dad belonged to them and their children (Genesis 31:16). Jacob immediately had his wives and children sit on camels and leave, traveling toward his father Isaac's home in Canaan. Jacob took all his flocks, herds, and other personal property he had gotten from northern Syria (Genesis 31:17–18) and what he owned. But before Rachel left, she went back to her father's home and stole the household idols while her dad was out caring for his sheep (Genesis 31:19, Judges 17:5). Jacob tricked his uncle Laban by not telling him or the Arameans he was leaving. Jacob traveled across the Euphrates River and headed for the hill country of Gilead (Genesis 31:20–21, 2 Kings 12:17).

Rachel and Leah must have been heartbroken having to leave their home without saying goodbye to their dad and brothers. The family separated because Uncle Laban was manipulating Jacob. Jacob was loyal and a hard worker but was not appreciated. His wives were in a constant battle trying to win his love. But in the end, the sisters supported one another and packed up and left with their husband, Jacob, and children.

Uncle Laban Catches Up with Jacob

Three days later, Uncle Laban found out that Jacob had left, and he traveled seven days before they found Jacob in the hill country of Gilead (Genesis 31:22–23). But before Uncle Laban saw Jacob, God appeared to him in a dream that night and warned him, "Do not threaten or promise Jacob" (Genesis 31:24, Job 33:15–16). So Jacob set up camp on one side of the hill country Gilead, and Uncle Laban and his relatives were on the other side of the hill country (Genesis 31:25).

Uncle Laban approached Jacob and said, "Look what you have done! You tricked me and ran off with my daughters like a kidnapper. Why did you sneak away without telling me?" Uncle Laban told Jacob he would have given him a going-away party with singing and music on tambourines and harps (Genesis 31:26, 1 Samuel 30:2). Uncle Laban complained about not having the chance to kiss his daughters and grandchildren goodbye. He felt Jacob was foolish (Genesis 31:27–28).

Uncle Laban told Jacob, "I understand you were eager to return to your father, but why did you have to steal my idols?" (Genesis 31:30).

Jacob replied, saying, "I left without notice because I was afraid you would take your daughters from me by force." Jacob told his uncle, "If you find anyone here with the idols, they will be killed and let his relative be a witness; please show me what belongs to you, and I will give it back" (Genesis 31:31–32). Laban searched Jacob's tents and his servant women's tent and could not find the idols. He started walking toward Rachel's tent, but she had already hidden the idols under the cushion she used as a saddle and sat on it. Laban looked everywhere and could not find the idols (Genesis 31:33–34).

Rachel quickly said, "Father, please do not be angry with me for not getting up; I am on my period" (Genesis 31:35, Leviticus 19:32).

Jacob became upset and angry and said to Uncle Laban,

What are you doing? What have I done
wrong? Have I committed a crime? Is this why

you are hunting me down? After you have searched through everything, did you find anything and if so, put it here so our relatives could see it. Then we can talk about what to do. After I worked hard for you for twenty years, not one of your sheep or goats had a miscarriage, and I had never eaten even one of your rams. (Genesis 31:37–38)

Jacob was so mad he was letting steam off his chest. He continued telling his uncle how much he suffered working for him. Jacob said,

If a wild animal killed one of your sheep or goats, I paid for it myself. And you demanded that I pay the full price! Whether it was day or night, I was responsible for the animals. I sweated every day and could not even get a good night's sleep because of the cold. I worked fourteen long years to earn your two daughters and another six years to buy your sheep. (Genesis 31:39–41, Exodus 22:10)

Jacob told his uncle, "If it were not for my grandfather, Abraham, and father, Isaac, worshiping God, I would have been doomed. You would have sent me anyway with nothing." But God saw Jacob's hard work and commitment and helped him. God even told Uncle Laban he was wrong (Genesis 31:42, Psalm 124:2).

I am proud of Jacob for telling his uncle how he felt; however, the mistake he made was allowing his uncle to take advantage of him for twenty years. Jacob should have set limits and boundaries from the beginning. Instead, he worked all those years with anger built up inside of him. He hated his uncle and cousins for the way he was treated and finally blew up. Do you have anger built up inside of you as Jacob had? If so, release it before it gets the best of you. Do not be stuck in that anger. It will come out eventually through your behavior as it did with Jacob. Finally, he had enough of getting bullied by a family member.

Jacob and Uncle Laban Make an Agreement

Uncle Laban told Jacob, "Leah and Rachel are my daughters, and their children belong to me. All those sheep you have are mine too." So everything Jacob had, his uncle felt they belong to him (Genesis 31:43). Laban had a lot of nerve even to think he could take Jacob's wives and children. God would not allow that to happen. But Laban realized there was nothing he could do to keep his daughters and their children. And because of that, Uncle Laban wanted to make peace with Jacob (Genesis 31:44).

They began to pile up some large rocks to remind themselves of the deal. So Jacob set up the large rock and told his men to gather more and pile them up. Then Jacob and his uncle ate a meal beside the rock (Genesis 31:45–46, Joshua 24:26–27). Laban named the pile of stones Jegar Sahadutha. But Jacob called it Galeed.

Uncle Laban said to Jacob, "This pile of rocks will remind us of our agreement." That was why the place was called Galeed (Genesis 31:47–48). Laban also said, "This pile of rocks means the Lord will watch us both while we are apart from each other." Therefore, the place was also called Mizpah (Genesis 31:49, Judges 11:29).

Uncle Laban was concerned about Jacob's future with his daughters. He said, "Jacob, if you mistreat my daughters or marry other women, I may not know about it, but remember, God is watching us!" (Genesis 31:50). Both piles of the rock and large rocks have been set for uncle Laban and Jacob as a reminder. Laban and Jacob agreed never to attack each other (Genesis 31:51–52).

Laban said, "My father Nahor, your grandfather Abraham, and their ancestors all worshiped the same God, and he will make sure that each of us keeps our agreement." Then Jacob made a promise in the name of the fearsome God his father Isaac had worshiped (Genesis 31:53). Jacob also killed an animal and offered it as a sacrifice there on the mountain, and he invited his men to eat with them.

After the meal, Uncle Laban and his relatives spent the night on the mountain, and early the following day, he kissed his daughters and grandchildren goodbye and went back home (Genesis 31:54–55). So the story ended up being positive at the end. Uncle Laban accepted Jacob's plan to go back home to where his father, Isaac, lived in Canaan. They both agreed, and God was their witness. God always had Jacob's best interest. He was just learning that God had his back. Do you believe God has your back? Do you trust him? Do you call on him only when you need him? It is getting late, grandkids. Until the next time.

Love,
Grandma

Thirty-Second Chapter Letter

Jacob Gets Ready to Meet
His Brother, Esau

Hello, grandkids. I hope you are in good spirits. Today is May 7, 2021. It is 4:30 p.m. I took off from writing a few days to reflect on Jacob's life journey. He was a humble and kind man. He never once complained about his living situation and work conditions. He said he slept in the cold and could not get a good night's sleep for twenty years. Yet he stayed focused and committed to his job while working with the flocks. In chapter 32 of Genesis, Jacob traveled back to his hometown where he last saw his parents, Isaac and Rebekah, and brother, Esau. In chapter letter 28, Jacob separated from his family. After all, his parents were afraid his brother, Esau, would kill him because he stole his firstborn rights and blessings. So they asked him to run to his uncle Laban's home for safety and to find a wife. After twenty years, he finally left Laban's house with his family to go back home.

Jacob was headed back home and knew he would have to face his brother, Esau. As he was on his way home, God's angels came and met him. When Jacob saw them, he said, "This is God's camp." So he named the place Mahanaim (Genesis 32:1–2, Numbers 22:31, Joshua 5:14). It is always best to settle your problems or issues beforehand instead of running away from them as Jacob did. But his parents influenced him to run because they were afraid for his life. In addition, his brother was an emotional man who said he would kill Jacob.

Because Jacob was not sure what would occur if he ran into his brother, he sent his men to see Esau first with a message, where he lived in the land of Seir, also known as Edom (Genesis 32:3). Jacob told his servants to say, "Master, I am your servant! I have lived with Uncle Laban all this time, and I own cattle, donkeys, and sheep, as well as servants" (Genesis 32:4–5, Proverbs 15:1). When the servant returned, they told Jacob that his brother was on his way to see him with his army of four hundred men. Jacob was frightened, so he divided his people, sheep, cattle, and camels, into two groups. He figured if his brother attacked one group, perhaps the others can escape (Genesis 32:6–8).

Jacob was so afraid he prayed to God and said,

> You, Lord, are the God who was worshiped by my grandfather Abraham and my father, Isaac. You told me to return home to my family, and you promised to be with me and make me successful. I do not deserve all the things you have blessed me with, your servant. I only had a walking stick, but now I have two large groups of people and animals. (Genesis 32:9–10, Psalm 50:15)

He pleaded with God to rescue him from his brother. Jacob's actions show how fearful he was. Jacob thought his brother would attack him, his wives, and his children (Genesis 32:11, Psalm 59:1–2). Jacob told God, "You have promised that I would be a success and that someday it will be as hard to count my descendants as it is to measure the stars in the sky" (Genesis 32:12). Jacob was so scared that he leaned on God for help. He knew God was the only one that could save his life.

Do you run from your problems as Jacob did? Are you afraid to reach out to your sibling or a family member that hurt or threaten you? Do you trust and believe God has your back? How often do you pray? Is it only when you need God? Jacob was not sure how God was going to help him. Prayer is powerful, and if you are running away from family problems, stop and ask God to give you the boldness to face your fears! And love your brother, sister, and family member. Life is too short. Jacob stayed away from his brother for twenty years because he feared his brother. And God knew this.

Jacob spent the night at the campsite, and the following day, he chose animals to give to his brother as a gift. He set aside two hundred female goats and twenty males, two hundred female sheep and twenty males, thirty female camels with their babies, forty cows and ten bulls, and twenty female donkeys and ten males (Genesis 32:14–15). Shortly after, Jacob put his servants in charge of each herd and instructed them to keep space between them (Genesis 32:16). He told the servant in charge of the first herd, "When Esau meets you, he will ask whose servant you are. He will want to know where you are going and who owns those animals you have" (Genesis 32:17). Next, Jacob told his servant to let his brother know that the animals belong to his servant Jacob and that he was sending them as a gift to his Master Esau (Genesis 32:18).

Jacob also told the second and third servants in charge of the herds to say the same thing when they met Esau. He also told them to make sure they let Esau know his brother, Jacob, followed them (Genesis 32:19). Jacob was hoping his brother would accept the gifts and be happy and happy to see him. The servants took the gifts ahead of Jacob, but he stayed behind and slept at the campsite (Genesis 32:20–21, Joshua 12:2, Numbers 21:24, Proverbs 21:14).

Jacob's Name Changed to Israel

Jacob could not sleep. He was thinking about his family's safety. So he got up in the middle of the night and took his wives, eleven children, and everything he owned across to the other side of the Jabbok River for safety (Genesis 32:22–23). Shortly after, Jacob went back to the campsite and spent the night alone. Jacob was trying to rest when a man started fighting him until daybreak. When the man saw Jacob was not giving in and winning the fight, the man struck

Jacob on the hip and threw it out of joint (Genesis 32:24–25, Hosea 12:2–4, 2 Corinthians 12:7). They kept wrestling until the man said,

> "Let go of me! It is almost daylight." Jacob said, "I will not let you go until you bless me." The man said, "Your name will no longer be Jacob. You have wrestled with God and with man, and you have won. That is why your name will be Israel." Jacob said, "Now tell me your name." "Don't you know who I am?" he asked. And he blessed Jacob. (Genesis 32:26–29, Judges 13:17)

I believe the spirit of God came to visit Jacob in his sleep because he knew Jacob was worried about his safety.

Jacob knew it was God because he said, "I have seen God face to face, and I am still alive." So Jacob named the place Peniel (Genesis 32:30). The sun was coming up when he left Peniel, limping because he was struck on the hip, and the muscle on his hip joint had been injured. That is why the people from Israel do not eat the hip muscle of any animal (Genesis 32:31–32).

What an experience Jacob had with the Spirit of God. He continued to wrestle with his emotions until he felt secure and confident God was with him. We will wrestle with our feelings and question if God is with us during our scary moments. But faith starts with us first. God will always be there for us, just as God did with me, as mentioned before. I wrestled within myself until God's Spirit instructed me to write this book. I believe people must sit still and allow the Spirit that lives in them to guide them to the next level. In terms of God, changing Jacob's name to Israel is a clear indication that his life will be changed from this point on. Sarah and Abraham's names were changed first in the Old Testament. I think God changed names in the Bible to establish their new character in the stories. It is getting late and time for me to close this letter. Until next time.

Love,
Grandma

Thirty-Third Chapter Letter

Jacob Meets His Brother, Esau

Good afternoon, grandkids. I hope you are doing well. Today is Thursday, May 13, 2021, and it is 1:00 p.m. This morning, I had my first vaccination shot. I did not feel anything. It has been 101 days I have been living with Grandma Josie. She continues to have good and bad days. She enjoys watering the front and back yards. I also play her favorite songs while we are outside. The music seems to send her down memory lane.

In the last letter, I shared what happened in Genesis, chapter 32. I explained how Jacob got himself and his family ready to meet his brother, Esau, in the previous note and how he wrestled with the Spirit of God and won! Jacob would not give up until he was blessed. He needed security and validation that God had his back. He refused to let go until he felt the confidence to let go, confident that God had his back! Once he felt free to let go, he was struck on his hip, and his name was changed to Israel. In this letter, I will discuss Jacob meeting his brother and traveling to Shechem in Canaan and setting up a campsite.

When Jacob was walking toward meeting his brother, Esau, he saw four hundred men following him. Jacob had his wives walk with their children—the two servant women, Zilpah and Bilhah, and their children, followed by Leah and her children, and then Rachel and Joseph following behind Jacob. In front of his family members, Jacob was bowing to the ground seven times as he walked toward his brother (Genesis 33:1–3). Esau saw his brother and immediately ran toward him and gave him a big hug and kiss. After that, the two brothers started crying (Genesis 33:4). I know Jacob was relieved his brother was not bitter.

Are you upset at a brother, sister, mother, or father? And have you not spoken to them in years because you think they are holding on to a grudge? Or is it you holding on to the past hurt? If so, it is time to let God and let go! Life is too short to hold on to old feelings. Please do not be stuck in your anger toward your family. You are doing what the devil wants. You are serving the devil's will, not what God would like for you.

When Esau saw Jacob's family, he asked, "Whose children are these?" Jacob replied, "These are the ones the Lord has been kind enough to give to me, your servant" (Genesis 33:5, Psalm 127:3, Isaiah 8:18). First, Jacob's two servant wives and their children walked up to Esau and bowed down to him. Secondly, Leah and her children bowed down to Esau. Finally, Joseph and Rachel walked up and bowed down to Esau (Genesis 33:6–7).

Esau asked Jacob, "What did you mean by these herds I met along the road?"

Jacob answered, "Master, I sent them so you would be friendly to me."

Esau said, "I have plenty, keep them for yourself" (Genesis 33:8–9).

Jacob said, "No! Please accept these gifts as a sign of our friendship for me." Jacob told his brother, "When you welcomed me, and I saw your face, it was like seeing God's face." He explained how God had been good to him and had given him everything he needed. However, Jacob would not stop insisting that his brother Esau take the gifts. Esau finally accepted the gifts (Genesis 33:10–11, 1 Samuel 25:27). God had blessed both with wealth.

Esau told his brother, Jacob, "Let us get ready to travel. I will go along with you."

Jacob answered, "Master, traveling is difficult for my children, and I have to look after the sheep and goats that are nursing their babies." Jacob told his brother he was concerned that if he traveled too much in one day, his flock would die. He suggested for Esau to go ahead and that he would travel slowly with his children and herds. Jacob and Esau agreed to meet in the country of Edom (Genesis 33:12–14). Esau was so kind he was willing to leave some of his men behind to help Jacob. But Jacob refused. Jacob said, "You do not have to do that; I am happy to build a house and set up a shelter for the flocks." He called it Succoth (Genesis 33:15–17, Joshua 13:27, Ruth 2:13, Joshua 13:27). Jacob was happy he and his brother reunited. I am sure they both felt good after twenty years. What a beautiful reunion.

Jacob Arrives at Shechem

Jacob left northern Syria and arrived safely at Shechem in Canaan and set up a campsite outside the city (Genesis 33:18, John 3:23). The camp where Jacob was staying was owned by the descendants of Hamor, the father of Shechem. So Jacob paid one hundred pieces of silver for the property, set up his tents, and built an altar to honor the God of Israel (Genesis 33:19–20, John 4:5). Recall Noah had three sons? His second son, Ham, is the ancestor of Hamor. They settled in Ethiopia, Egypt, Put, and Canaan (Genesis 10:6, 1 Chronicles 1:8). And Canaan's sons were Sidon and Heth, the ancestor of the Hivites, Hamor, the father of Shechem.

I think Jacob was concerned for his flocks and children traveling for long days, so he decided to stop at Shechem for they could settle and regroup. After all, he was carrying a heavy heart and worried about his brother hurting him and his family. I must close now and get Grandma Josie dinner together. Until the following letter.

Love,
Grandma

Thirty-Fourth Chapter Letter

Leah's Daughter Is Raped

Greetings, grandkids. I hope you are doing well. Today is Thursday, May 13, 2021. I decided to pick up where I left off a few hours ago. I will be talking about what happened in Genesis, chapter 34. In the last letter, Jacob met up with his brother, Esau. They both cried and were happy to see each other. Later, Jacob traveled to Shechem and bought land from Hamor outside the city of Shechem in Canaan. Just a reminder, Jacob's roots come from Noah's son, Shem, the older brother of Japheth (Genesis 10:21). Shem had a son named Nahor, who had a son named Terah. Terah became Abraham's father (Genesis 11:26). Abraham is Jacob's grandfather. I just want to point out the roots of the characters. They are descendants of Noah's three sons. They are all related, cousins, uncles, aunts, and grandparents.

Recall Jacob's first wife is Leah. They had six sons and one daughter named Dinah. The story begins with Jacob, Leah, and their daughter visiting women who lived in the land. Shechem, the leader of the Hivites, saw how beautiful Dinah was and grabbed and raped her. Shechem was so attracted to Dinah because she was lovely. He told Dinah how much he loved her. Then Shechem asked his father, Hamor, to ask her father, Jacob, to give her to be his wife (Genesis 34:2–4, Judges 14:2). Jacob heard what had happened but did not do anything at that moment. Her brothers were out in the field working with the cattle.

Hamor visited Jacob at his home, and while he was there, Jacob's sons were coming in from work. When they heard about their sister being raped, they were furious. Nothing is more disgraceful than rape, and it should not be tolerated in Israel (Genesis 34:5–7, 2 Samuel 13:22, Judges 20:6). This is the first rape story in the Bible. However, not the first in the world today.

Hamor spoke to Jacob and his sons about his son Shechem. He explained how much in love he is with Dinah. Hamor said to Jacob and his sons, "Please let my son marry her. Why don't you start letting your families marry into our families and our families marry into yours" (Genesis 34:8–9)? Hamor tried his best to convince Jacob that they could share his land if he allowed his daughter to get married. And they could "move around freely until they saw a part of the land they liked and purchased it from him" (Genesis 34:10). Shechem said, "Do this favor for me, and I will give whatever you want. I will do anything to marry Dinah" (Genesis 34:11–12). What is interesting in the story is that they are family, and they do not know. They come from Shem and Ham, who are brothers, Noah's sons. But how would they know their history? I guess they would not know that because their ancestors were separated when God told them to go out and populate the world after the flood (Genesis 9:7). They were scattered all over the earth (Genesis 11:8). They had their tribes, languages, and land (Genesis 10:2). I do not even know which of Noah's sons is my relative. All I know is it started with Noah's three sons.

Jacob's sons wanted to get even with Shechem and his father because of what happened to their sister (Genesis 34:13, Exodus 8:29, 2 Samuel 13:24). So the brothers played a trick on them by saying, "You guys are not circumcised! And it would be a disgrace for us to let you marry our sister now. However, we will let you marry her if you and the other men in your tribe get circumcised. Then your family can marry into ours, and ours can marry into yours, and we can live together like one nation" (Genesis 34:14–16, Exodus 12:48, Joshua 5:9). The brothers told them if they chose not to do what they are requesting, they would take their sister, Dinah, and leave (Genesis 34:17).

Hamor and Shechem liked what was said. Shechem was very respectful toward Jacob and his sons because he loved Dinah and wanted to marry her, so he immediately left to get done what was requested (Genesis 34:18–19, 1 Chronicles 4:9). Hamor and Shechem shared what needed to be done with their servants (Genesis 34:20, Ruth 4:1). Hamor told his men that Jacob and his family were friendly people. "I do not see why it would be a problem for Jacob's family to move on our property," said Hamor. "They can move around freely until they find the property they want. There is enough land here for them and us. Then our families can marry into theirs, and theirs can marry into ours" (Genesis 34:21).

Hamor said, "We have to do only one thing before they agree to stay here and become one nation with us." Every man in Shechem had to be circumcised like Jacob's men (Genesis 34:22). Hamor was thinking, "We will get their property, as well as their flocks and herds. All we have to do is agree to get circumcised, and they will live with us" (Genesis 34:23). Every grown man followed Hamor and Shechem's request and got circumcised (Genesis 34:24).

Hamor's tribe were nonbelievers, pagan people. If they were godly people, they would have been circumcised. Recall being circumcised was a covenant between God and his believers in Abraham, Isaac, and Jacob's days. Instead, Hamor had other things on his mind, like gaining Jacob's wealth. He looked at his goods and wanted some of the flocks and herds. Greed entered his mind instead of being satisfied with what he had. And his son raping Dinah was a sin. Her brothers had every right to be upset!

Dinah's Brothers Retaliated

The men from Shechem were circumcised, and three days later, they were still in pain (Genesis 34:25). Two of Dinah's brothers Simeon and Levi, attacked the men with their swords and killed every man in the town, including Hamor and Shechem, and they took their sister and left (Genesis 34:26). Then Jacob's other sons came and took everything they wanted. The brothers wanted revenge for what happened to their sister (Genesis 34:27). The brothers took sheep, goats, donkeys, and everything that was in the fields. They also went into their houses, stole everything valuable, and dragged their wives and children (Genesis 34:28–29).

Jacob found out what Simeon and Levi did and said, "Look what you have done! Now I will be in real trouble with the Canaanites and Perizzites who live near here. We are few, and if they attack us, they will kill everyone in my household." The sons answered, "Was it right to let our sister be treated that way?" (Genesis 34:30–31, Proverbs 6:34, Leviticus 19:29).

Dinah's brother's killing Hamor and his son and others in their tribe was unacceptable and sinful. Killing people is never the right way to handle any situation. As mentioned before, Hamor's ancestors come from Ham, one of Noah's sons. And Jacob's ancestors come from Shem, one of Noah's sons. I am not sure if they knew their ancestors or if they were related. The Bible does not say. But I am almost certain they are relatives. However, Jacob was upset at his two sons, Simeon and Levi, for killing Hamor and his people. He did not say too much to his sons about the situation, but they will soon have to deal with their consequences.

I must close now. God bless you and be safe. Until the following letter.

Love,
Grandma

Thirty-Fifth Chapter Letter

Jacob Returns to Bethel

Good morning, grandkids. I hope all is well. Today is May 14, 2021. I am doing well, and so is Grandma Josie. The last letter I shared with you was about Dinah being raped and how her two brothers got revenge by killing every male in Hamor's tribe, including Hamor and his son. Jacob was so upset at his sons, Simeon and Levi, for killing these people but did not talk about it further with his sons.

The sons felt it was not right for their sister to be raped. God knew everything that took place in the city of Shechem in Canaan. And because of that, he instructed Jacob to return to Bethel where "I appeared to you when you were running from your brother Esau." God told Jacob to go make his home there and "build an altar for me" (Genesis 35:1). Shortly after, Jacob told everyone traveling with them to get rid of all their foreign gods! Their foreign gods could be anything from charms, necklets, earrings, idols, and a statue. In my opinion, a foreign god could be anything the separates you from our Lord Jesus Christ. Jacob told everyone to make themselves acceptable to worship God and wear clean clothes (Genesis 35:2, Joshua 24:15).

Shortly after, Jacob told them they were going to travel to Bethel. Jacob said he would build an altar there for God, who had answered all his prayers when he was in trouble and who has always had his back! Finally, Jacob acknowledged that God had been holding his hand one step at a time! He knew God rescued him and his family from the tragic killings his sons did. I cannot express enough about the power of prayer. I pray when I feel I do not have control over a situation or when I see trouble coming my way, and I always give thanks to God! God is real and knows your problems before you face them. Ask for help. He wants us to depend on him for his guidance.

After Jacob talked to the people regarding their idols, he told them they would be traveling to Bethel, and he would build an altar there for God who answered his prayers when he was in trouble and always had his back (Genesis 35:3).

Everyone listened to Jacob and gave him their idols and earrings, and he buried them under an oak tree near Shechem (Genesis 35:4, Hosea 2:13). When Jacob and his family traveled through Canaan, God previously contacted the townspeople and told them not to bother him or his family. God terrified them. When they reached Bethel, also known as Luz, Jacob built an altar there and called it "God of Bethel" because that is when God had appeared to him when he was running from his brother Esau (Genesis 35:5–7). And when they were there in town, Rebekah's servant Deborah died. She was buried under an oak tree, and they called it "Weeping Oak" (Genesis 34:8).

I cannot stress enough to find a special place in your home environment inside or out and dedicate that place to God to give him thanks. We all need a quiet place to pray and meditate. Always take time out and give God the glory as Jacob did. Jacob was a great role model for the people and us.

God Blesses Jacob at Bethel

When Jacob was back in the land of Canaan, God appeared to him again. God told Jacob he would give him a new name and was going to bless him by saying, "I am God All-Powerful, and from now on, your name will be Israel instead of Jacob. You will have many children. Your descendants will become nations, and some of the men in your family will even be kings" (Genesis 35:9–11, Daniel 10:5, Hosea 12:4, Joshua 5:13). God said, "I will give you the land that I promised Abraham and Isaac, and it will belong to your family forever (Genesis 35:12). God left after talking to Jacob (Genesis

35:13). Jacob then set up a large rock so that he would remember what had happened there. Jacob poured wine and olive oil on the rock to show that it was dedicated to God, and he named the place Bethel (Genesis 35:14–15).

Benjamin Is Born

Jacob and his family left Bethel and were a long way from Bethlehem Ephrath. Rachel was pregnant and was having a difficult time traveling. Her baby was soon to be born. Her servant told her not to worry, that she would have a boy (Genesis 35:16–17, Ruth 4:11, Micah 5:2)! Rachel was close to dying, and right before she died, she said, "I will name him Benoni." But Jacob chose to name his son Benjamin (Genesis 35:18). Rachel was buried beside the road to Bethlehem Ephrath. After that, Ephrath is called Bethlehem (Genesis 35:19). Jacob set up a tombstone over her grave, still there (Genesis 35:20, 1 Samuel 10:2). Jacob, known as Israel, continued traveling to the south of Eder Tower, where he set up a campsite (Genesis 35:21, Micah 4:8). During this time, Jacob's oldest son, Reuben, slept with his wife, Bilhah, who was Rachel's servant. And Jacob found out (Genesis 35:22, Genesis 49:4, 1 Chronicles 5:1). And because he slept with one of his wives, he lost his rights as the firstborn son (1 Chronicles 5:1). And Ruben lost his power as a first-born son.

People who sleep around with family members, wives, or husbands will pay for their mistakes. It is not worth the family separation, pain, and lost time.

Jacob's Twelve Sons

Jacob had twelve sons while living in northern Syria. The following list outlines Jacob's first wife, Leah, who had six sons: Reuben, Simeon, Levi, Judah, Issachar, and Zebulun. In addition, Leah's servant, Zilpah, had two sons named Gad and Asher.

Jacob's wife, Rachel, had two sons named Joseph and Benjamin. Rachel's servant, named Bilhah, had two sons named Dan and Naphtali (Genesis 35:23–26). Jacob had four wives and twelve sons.

Isaac Dies

Jacob visited his father, Isaac, at Hebron, known as Mamre or Kiriath-Arba, where Isaac lived as a foreigner (Genesis 35:27). He was old and died at 180, and his sons Esau and Jacob buried him (Genesis 35:28–29, Proverbs 6:34, Leviticus 19:29). I will close this letter now. Until next time.

Love,
Grandma

Thirty-Sixth Chapter Letter

Esau's Family

Good morning, grandkids. I hope you are doing well and staying in prayer. Today is Tuesday, May 18, 2021. It is 10:50 a.m. Grandma and I just finished breakfast, and I wanted to get back to writing you all. In the last chapter, God told Jacob to go back "home and build a home there and an altar for me" (Genesis 35:1). When Jacob arrived in Bethlehem, God blessed him. Benjamin was born, and his mother, Rachel, died and was buried along the side of the road in Bethlehem. And I listed Jacob's twelve sons by name and their mothers. Finally, the story ended with Isaac dying and his sons burying him. In Genesis, chapter 36, forty-three Bible verses are outlined with Esau's wives, sons, and grandsons and Edomite chiefs and leaders. I will only list Esau's sons and grandsons. I will only write the names of Esau's immediate family members and not the chiefs and leaders of the Edomites from Genesis 36:15–43. I do not think it is necessary.

Esau is known as Edom, and he had many descendants (Genesis 36:1). He married three Canaanite women. Recall the Canaanites are the descendants of Ham, Noah's son. Ham had a son, Canaan, who had a son named Heth (Genesis 10). Esau's first wife was Adah, the daughter of Elon the Hittite, and his second wife was Oholibamath, the daughter of Anah and the granddaughter of Zibeon the Hivite (Genesis 36:2). His third wife was Basemath, Ishmael's daughter and Nebaioth's sister (Genesis 36:3). Recall Ishmael was Abraham's first son with the Egyptian woman named Hagar, Sarah's servant. So can you see that family members are marrying their extended families, although they come from different tribes?

Esau and his three wives had a total of five sons while they lived in Canaan. Adah, Esau's first wife, had a son named Eliphaz. The second wife, Basemath, had a son named Reuel. And Oholibamah had three sons, Jeush, Jalam, and Korah (Genesis 36:4–5, 1 Chronicles 1:35). Esau took his wives, relatives, servants, animals, and possessions he earned while in Canaan and moved far away from his brother Jacob (Genesis 36:6). He moved away because the land they were sharing was too small and crowded. In addition, Esau could not support his family, nor his brother, Jacob, with all his flocks and herds. So he moved and made his home in the hills of the country of Seir (Genesis 36:7–8, Deuteronomy 2:5).

Esau lived in the hill country of Seir and was the ancestor of the Edomites. These three wives—Adah, Basemath, Oholibamah—and their descendants are listed in the following order: Esau and Adah had a son named Eliphaz. His sons were named Teman, Omar, Zepho, Gatam, and Kenaz. Eliphaz married a woman named Timna, and they had a son named Amalek (Genesis 36:9–14, 1 Chronicles 1:35, Exodus 17:8–14, Numbers 24:20, 1 Samuel 15:2).

Esau and his second wife had a son named Reuel, who had Nahath, Zerah, Shammah, and Mizzah.

Esau and his third wife, Oholibamah, only had three sons: Jeush, Jalam, and Korah (Genesis 36:9–14). Nevertheless, God blessed Esau with a big family and wealth. So even though his parents were against marrying women from the Canaan tribe, he was happy and prospered and forgot about being angry at his brother Jacob. I am going to close now and will see you in the following letter. Goodnight!

Love,
Grandma

Thirty-Seventh Chapter Letter

Joseph and His Brothers

Greetings, grandkids. I hope you are doing well and trying to live your lives with love for people. As for me, I am still taking care of Grandma Josie. She sleeps most nights, so I have decided to go home and sleep in my bed after one hundred and five days. I leave at 9:30 p.m. and return at 8:00 a.m. before she wakes up. This allows me to do a few things in my home and spend time with Papa. In the last letter, I shared a list of Esau's family members, including his three Canaanite wives. Esau is known as Edom, the father of the Edomites. They adopted this name from where they settled (Genesis 26:43). In this next chapter of Genesis, chapter 37, I will write about Jacob and his family's lives in Canaan. This letter will focus on Jacob's twelve sons, especially Joseph, who was treated harshly by his older brothers. As mentioned before, Jacob had twelve sons and one daughter.

Jacob lived in Canaan, where his father, Isaac, had lived. I will be sharing their family's story (Genesis 37:1, 1 Samuel 2:22). When Jacob's younger son Joseph was seventeen years old, he cared for sheep with his stepbrothers in the fields, and their mothers were the servants of Leah and Rachel named Bilhah and Zilpah. Joseph always told his father, Jacob, negative things about his brothers (Genesis 37:2, 1 Samuel 2:22–24). Nevertheless, his parent treated Joseph special, and he knew it. Unfortunately, his older brothers could not hold back their jealousy toward him. If you are ever in a situation like Joseph's brothers, treat your stepsibling with love. Jealousy does not get you anywhere, and the devil loves conflict between family members. Do not let him win!

Jacob loved Joseph more than his other sons because he was born in his old age and knew he was a blessing. However, one day, Jacob had given his son Joseph a fancy coat to show him he was the favorite son, and because of that, his brothers hated him and treated him rudely (Genesis 37:3–4).

One day, Joseph and his brothers were out working, and he told them what he had dreamed, and they hated him even more (Genesis 37:5). So he said, "Let me tell you about my dream. We were out in the field, tying up bundles of wheat. Suddenly my bundle stood up, and your bundles gathered around and bowed down to it" (Genesis 37:6–7). So his brothers said, "Do you think you are going to be king and rule over us?" And because of the dream, his brothers hated Joseph for what he said (Genesis 37:8, Deuteronomy 33:16). So Joseph had another dream and told his brothers to listen to his vision. "The sun, the moon, and eleven stars bowed down to me." When Joseph told his father, Jacob, about his dream, he became agitated and said, "What is that supposed to mean? Are your mother and I and your brothers all going to come and bow down in front of you" (Genesis 37:9–10)? Joseph's brothers got even more jealous of him, and his father, Jacob, did not understand why he was having these dreams and wondered about them (Genesis 37:11, Acts 7:9).

Has God ever shared a vision in your dreams? He has with me many times. But I do not know at that moment what they meant until I experience what I have dreamed. I think Jacob knew there was a profound message in Joseph's dream but could not put his finger on it. Jacob wondered about Joseph's dreams.

Joseph Is Sold by His Brothers and Taken to Egypt

Joseph's brothers were out taking sheep to a pasture near Shechem when their father, Jacob, requested Joseph to go out and check on his brothers. "I want you to go to your brothers. They are with the sheep near Shechem." Joseph replied, "Yes sir." (Genesis 37:12–13). Jacob then told Joseph to see how his brothers are doing with the sheep and come back and let him know. So he left from Hebron Valley. When Joseph was near Shechem, he wandered off through the fields when a man saw him and asked, "Who are you looking for?" (Genesis 37:14–15). Joseph answered, "I am looking for my brothers who are watching the sheep. Can you tell me where they are?" The man said, "I overheard them say they were going to Dothan." So Joseph left and went to Dothan and located his brothers (Genesis 37:16–17, Song of Songs 1:7, 2 King 6:13). They saw him coming toward them and talked about planning to kill him. They said to one another, "Here comes the hero of those dreams" (Genesis 37:18–19, 1 Samuel 19:1, Mark 14:1). "Let us kill him and throw him into a pit and say that a wild animal ate him. And then we will see what happens to the dreams" (Genesis 37:20; Proverbs 1:11).

Reuben, the oldest brother, overheard his other brothers plotting and tried to stop them. Reuben told his brothers not to kill him. He said, "Do not murder him or even harm him. Just throw him into a dry well out here in the desert." Reuben did not want to harm Joseph. He figured he could go back and get Joseph if he were tossed in the well and then take him back to their father (Genesis 37:21–22). When Joseph approached his brothers, they pulled off his fancy coat and threw him into a dry well (Genesis 37:23–24, Matthew 27:28).

As they were in town eating, they looked up and saw a caravan of Ishmaelites coming from Gilead. Their camels were loaded with spices that they were taking to Egypt (Genesis 37:25, Jeremiah 8:22). Judah then said, "What will we gain if we kill our brother and hide his body? Let us sell him to the Ishmaelites and not harm him. After all, he is our brother" (Genesis 37:26–27, 1 Samuel 18:17). The brothers agreed. Reuben was not there when his brothers had the conversation and when they sold Joseph. When the Midianite merchants came by, the brothers pulled Joseph out of the well and sold him for twenty pieces of silver to the Ishmaelites, who took him to Egypt (Genesis 37:28, Judges 6:1–2). Recall the Ishmaelites are Ishmael's tribal people. Ishmael was the son of the Egyptian woman Hagar, Sarah's servant, who was Abraham's first son. Who is Jacob's grandfather? Can you see how these people are all related?

Reuben returned to the well looking for Joseph; he could not find him. He was so hurt he tore his clothes in sorrow. Reuben went back to where his brothers were and said, "The boy is gone! What am I going to do" (Genesis 37:28–30, Job 1:20)? The brothers killed a goat and dipped Joseph's fancy coat in the blood. Then they took the coat to their father, Jacob, and asked him to look closely to see if it belonged to his son Joseph (Genesis 37:31–32). Jacob immediately knew the coat belonged to his son Joseph. He said, "It is my son's coat! Joseph had been torn to pieces and eaten by some wild animals" (Genesis 37:33).

Jacob mourned for Joseph for a long time, and to show his sorrow, he tore his clothes and wore sackcloth (Genesis 37:34). Jacob's other sons tried to comfort him, but he refused to be comforted. So finally, he said, "No! I will go to my grave, mourning for my son." So Jacob kept mourning (Genesis 37:35, 2 Samuel 12:17). The Midianites eventually sold Joseph in Egypt to a man named Potiphar, the king's official in charge of the palace guard (Genesis 37:36).

I cannot believe how Joseph's older brothers harmed him because of the jealousy and anger they had built up toward him! They were jealous of his relationship with their dad and about the dreams he shared. Could it have been because they had different mothers? Or because Jacob treated this youngest son special? Rueben, on the other hand, the most senior of them all, was the only one that seemed to show remorse. Even though he did not take leadership and intervene to help his brother Joseph, they were all wrong. However, Judah did step up and say to his brothers, "Let us not kill or hurt our brother; after all, he is our brother."

Their father, Jacob, was a faithful and humble man. He honored God and worshiped him wherever he went. Jacob's twelve sons witnessed their father's love for God, yet they forgot. Their jealousy and anger toward Joseph blinded their faith. Has that ever happened to you when you were angry?

"When the governor's soldiers led Jesus into the fortress and brought together the rest of the troops, they stripped off Jesus's clothes and put a scarlet robe on him" (Matthew 27:27–28). "And after they finished making fun of Jesus, they took off his robe"

(Matthew 27:31), just like Joseph's brother oppressed him and took off his robe.

I will close for now, and I hope you understood the message in this part of the story. Until next time.

Love you,
Grandma

Thirty-Eighth Chapter Letter

Judah and Tamar

Good afternoon, my grandkids. I hope you are doing well. As for Grandma Josie and me, we are well. Today is May 21, 2021. It is 2:00 p.m. I am overly excited to continue writing about Jacob and his son's life. In the last letter, I shared how Joseph told his father, Jacob, and his brothers about his dreams, and they became very jealous and angry toward him because of that. But Jacob treated Joseph special because he felt it was a blessing from God to have a son at his old age. So Joseph's brothers tossed him in a dry well and eventually sold him to a man from Egypt named Potiphar, a king's official in charge of the palace guard.

In this following letter, I will be writing about what happened in Genesis 38. The story in chapter 38 talks about Leah's son Judah and how he left the family on the hill and lived near a friend in the town of Adullam. He got married and had three sons. Then he ran into a woman and thought she was a prostitute, had sex with her, and later found out it was his daughter-in-law. After that, the story gets more interesting. However, Joseph will not be mentioned in this letter.

Judah left his home in the hill country and went to live near his friend Hirah in the town of Adullam (Genesis 38:1, 2 Kings 4:8). While he was there, he met Shua's daughter, who was Canaanite. "Judah married her, and they had three sons" (Genesis 38:2–3). Her son's name was, Er, the second was called Onan, and the third was named Shelah. Judah was in Chezib when her third son was born (Genesis 38:4–5, Numbers 26:19–20). When Judah's first son, Er, grew up, he chose a woman to marry him. Unfortunately, Er was an angry and evil man, so the Lord took his life (Genesis 38:6–7). And because he lost this life, his father Judah had his second son Onan marry Er's wife. So Judah told Onan, "You have to marry Tamar and have a child for your brother" (Genesis 38:8). However, Onan was not feeling his dad's request. But he went along with it. Onan knew she was not his wife, and it was his dead brother's wife. So when he had sex with Tamar, he made sure she would not get pregnant. The Lord knew what was going on and disapproved of his behavior and took his life (Genesis 38:8–10, Deuteronomy 25:5–6). Judah did not want his third son, Shelah, to die, so he told Tamar to "go home to your father and live there as a widow until my son Shelah is grown." So Tamar went to live with her father (Genesis 38:11, Ruth 1:12).

Tamar Tricks Judah

Years later, Judah's wife died, and he mourned for her. He kept busy by visiting his friend Hirah in the town of Timnah, where sheep were being sheared (Genesis 38:12, 2 Samuel 13:39). Shearing is when the sheep's wool is getting cut, like a haircut. Tamar, Judah's daughter-in-law, heard that her father-in-law was coming to Timnah to get his sheep sheared (Genesis 38:13, Joshua 15:10). Tamar knew that Judah's son Shelah was grown but was not allowed to marry her. So she decided to trick Judah and dressed up in a different type of clothing that had a veil to cover her face rather than wearing her widow clothes. After she dressed up, she sat outside the town of Enaim on the side of the road going toward Timash (Genesis 38:14, Proverbs 7:12). Tamar was behaving like a prostitute. She had one thing on her mind, to have sex and get pregnant since they would not allow her to marry Shelah.

When Judah traveled along the road, he did not recognize Tamar because her face was covered. Therefore, Judah thought she was a prostitute (Genesis 38:15). Even if she was not, she was act-ing like a prostitute. Judah asked her to sleep with him. She asked Judah,

> "What will you give me if I do?" Judah replied, "One of my young goats." She said, "What would you give me to keep until you send me the goat?" Judah said, "What do you want?" She said, "The ring on the cord you have around your neck and the special walking stick you have with you." He gave her whatever she asked for, and she slept with him and got pregnant. (Genesis 38:16–18, Judges 15:1, Ezekiel 16:33)

Judah had his friend Hirah take the goat to Tamar so that she could give him back the ring and walking stick, but his friend could not find her when he went back looking for her (Genesis 38:19–20). So Hirah asked around the town of Enaim for the prostitute. He said, "Where is the prostitute who sat along the road outside your town?" The people said, "There's never been one here in this town" (Genesis 38:21, Hosea 4:14). Judah was headed for a big surprise. Dealing with a prostitute is no joke. God is against this type of behavior. The devil loves when men or women get caught up in prostitution because you are serving him. It is a trap and not worth it.

Hirah went back to share with Judah that he could not find the prostitute. He told Judah what the townspeople said; no prostitute had ever been there (Genesis 38:22). Judah said, "If you could not find her, we will just let her keep the things I gave her. And we will forget about the goat because we will look like fools" (Genesis 38:23).

Three months later, someone told Judah that his daughter-in-law Tamar was behaving like a prostitute and now she is pregnant. Judah was so mad he shouted, "Drag her out of town and burn her to death" (Genesis 38:24, Judges 19:2)! As Tamar was being pulled out, she told the servant to show her father-in-law that the man who gave her the ring and walking stick was the one who got her pregnant. Judah saw the items and said, "Those are mine!" Then Judah admitted he slept with her.

He said she was a better person than he was because he broke his promise to let her marry his son Shelah. After that, Judah never touched her again (Genesis 38:25–26). She later gave birth to twins. But before they were born, one of them stuck a hand out of her womb.

> The woman who was helping her tied a red thread around the baby's hand and explained, "This one came out first." Immediately, the hand went back in, and the other child was born first. The servant that was helping said, "What an opening you have made for yourself!" So, they named the baby Perez, and when the brother came out, the red thread came out, and he was named Zerah. (Genesis 38:27–30, Numbers 26:20, Matthew 1:3, 1 Chronicles 2:4)

There were a lot of twists and turns in this story with Judah and Tamar.

The twins in Tamar's stomach remind me of Isaac's twins, Esau and Jacob. Recall their mother Rebekah praying and asking God why her babies were fighting in her stomach. God said because "your two sons will become two separated nations. The younger one will be his servant" (Genesis 25:23). In Tamar's situation, one of her babies stuck a hand out of her womb. Her servant tied a red thread around his hand and said, "This one came out first," but right away, the hand went back in, and the other child was born first. The baby was named Perez, which means "Breach." It may mean the twins may have conflicts like Esau and Jacob. My ancestor's name is Perez. My grandfather was Pedro Perez.

Tamar wanted children, so she did whatever she could to have them. Judah thought he could get away with sleeping with a prostitute and got caught. You will always get caught when your intentions are wrong. As mentioned before, whatever goes on in the dark will always come to light. Judah lied to Tamar and told her she could marry his son Shelah when he was old enough, but he would not allow that to happen because he was afraid of losing another son. Back in those days, it was customary to marry a brother's wife if he died to carry the name.

Judah, on the other hand, ended up being a chosen man by his father, Jacob. Jacob blessed him and appointed him a leader among the twelve brothers (Genesis 49:8–10). He was promised that he would be the ancestor of the Messiah by his father, Jacob, and the founder of the tribe of Judah, the line of King David and Jesus Christ (Matthew 1:3–16). Thus, Christ is called the "Lion of the tribe of Judah" (Revelation 5:5).

Grandkids, I am going to close this letter. It is getting late. Until the next time.

Love,
Grandma

Thirty-Ninth Chapter Letter

Joseph and Potiphar's Wife

Greetings, grandkids. I hope you are all doing well and staying out of trouble. Today is Sunday, May 23, 2021. It is 6:25 p.m. The last letter I wrote talked about Judah and Tamar's relationship and how Judah's two sons died because they were evil and refused to follow their dad's request to have children with Tamar. Instead, she tricked him, and as a result, had twin boys. In this following letter, I will share what happened in Genesis, chapter 39. Recall Joseph's brothers sold him to the Ishmaelites, who later sold him to an official in charge of the palace guard in Egypt (Genesis 39:1). Joseph lived in the home of Potiphar, his Egyptian owner (Genesis 39:2–3, Acts 7:9, Psalm 1:3).

Potiphar liked Joseph and made him his assistant and put him in charge of his house and property (Genesis 39:4). Potiphar saw how God had blessed his family and land because of Joseph. Potiphar did not have to do anything but order his food. Joseph was a very handsome man with a nice build (Genesis 39:5–6, 1 Samuel 16:12). Potiphar's wife had her eye on Joseph. She asked him to make love to her, but he refused and said, "My master is not worried about anything in his house because he has me in charge of everything he owns" (Genesis 39:7–8, 2 Samuel 13:11). Joseph told Potiphar's wife that no one in the master's house was more important than he was and that the only thing he had not given him was his wife because he was married to her. Joseph told her he would not sin against God

(Genesis 39:9, Proverbs 6:29). She kept begging him to have sex with her every day, but he refused and would not get close to her (Genesis 39:10, Proverbs 1:10).

One day, Joseph went to do some work at Potiphar's house and realized none of the servants were around when suddenly, Potiphar's wife grabbed him, held on to his coat, and said, "Make love to me!" Joseph immediately ran out of the house, trying to get away from Potiphar's wife, and accidentally left his coat while trying to get away. She wanted to hold him back from going (Genesis 39:11–12, Proverbs 7:13). However, she was so mad and angry at Joseph for not wanting to make love to her she called in her servants and said, "Look! This Hebrew has come just to make fools of us. He tried to rape me, but I screamed for help. He heard me screaming and ran off, leaving his coat with me" (Genesis 39:13–15). Potiphar's wife kept Joseph's coat so she could show her husband when he came home. When he arrived, she told him that "the Hebrew servant you have tried to rape me! And when I screamed for help, he dropped his coat and ran out of the house" (Genesis 39:16–18, Exodus 23:1).

Potiphar became so angry at Joseph that he ordered Joseph be sent to prison with other prisoners (Genesis 39:19, Proverbs 6:34). However, when Joseph was in prison, the Lord helped him and was good to him; God even made the jailers put him in charge of the other prisoners and everything needed in jail (Genesis 39:20–22, Psalm 105:18–22, Acts 7:9). Therefore, the jailers did not worry about anything because they knew God was watching over Joseph and made him successful in all he did (Genesis 39:23). Thus, God was faithful to Joseph, and Joseph was faithful to God! We can have that same kind of relationship with God because he loves us unconditionally.

Have you ever been approached by a friend's wife or husband to have a sexual relationship? Or are you having an adulterous relationship? If so, get out of it immediately! And ask God to forgive you. It is not worth the consequences. It is better to run like Joseph. He refused and passed God's test. The devil loves this type of behavior, and God is against adultery. In God's Ten Commandments, it states, "Thou shall not commit adultery" (Exodus 20:14).

It was the second time Joseph faced a situation where his coat was taken from him. Recall the coat removed from him by his jealous brothers? And now in this situation, Joseph's coat was taken by Potiphar's wife, and she used it to frame him. I think the wife was mad because Joseph rejected her. He refused to fall into her sexual desires. Joseph did not want to disappoint God during the challenging moment because he said, "I do not want to sin against God." That is a powerful line we all can use under stressful situations!

I am going to end this letter this evening. Until the following letter.

Love,
Grandma

Fortieth Chapter Letter

Joseph Tells the Meaning of the Prisoners' Dreams

Good morning, grandkids, it is May 26, 2021, and it's 8:37 a.m. I am so excited about this book. I hope you can see how the stories in Genesis reflect the same issues in many families today in our world. Family separation is not God's will for us. The following ten chapter letters will center on Joseph and his brothers' family struggles. However, God never left Joseph's side through his trials and tribulations, and he will never leave us!

In the last letter, I shared Joseph's encounter with Potiphar's wife. She tried to get Joseph to have sex with her, but he refused and ran away. When Potiphar heard about the situation, he put Joseph in prison. In this letter, I will write what happened in Genesis 40. Joseph ended up serving other prisoners and interpreting their dreams. The king's servant and chief cook made him mad, so he put both of them in the same prison with Joseph (Genesis 40:1–3, Nehemiah 1:11, Proverbs 16:14). As a result, they all spent a long time in prison together, and Potiphar, the official in charge of the palace guard, made Joseph serve the chief cook and the king's servant (Genesis 40:4).

The cook and the servant had a dream one night, but their dreams were different. They talked about it but could not figure out what the dreams meant. When Joseph served the two men the following day, he could tell they were upset about something and asked what they were worried about (Genesis 40:5–7, Nehemiah 2:2). They replied, "We each had a dream last night, and there is no one that could tell us what they mean." So Joseph said, "God knows the meaning of the dreams. Tell me what you two dreamed" (Genesis 40:8). Joseph's relationship with God was so deep that God blessed him with the wisdom to interpret dreams. We too can have that same relationship with our Lord Jesus Christ. It was an excellent opportunity for the cook and the king's servant to ask about God.

When you ever have a chance to tell people about God, do not ever hesitate to share God's word and how he has blessed you, as Joseph did.

The king's servant told Joseph, "In my dream, I saw a vine with three branches. As soon as it budded, it blossomed, and its grapes became ripe. I then held the cup and squeezed the grapes into it, then I gave it to the king" (Genesis 40:9–11).

Joseph said, "This is the meaning of your dream. The three branches stand for three days, and in three days, the king will pardon you. After that, he will make you his servant again, and you will serve his wine, just like you used to do" (Genesis 40:12–13, Daniel 2:36, 2 Kings 25:27). "When these things happen when you go back to work for the king, do not forget to tell him about me," Joseph said. "I was kidnapped. Here in Egypt, I have not done anything to deserve being tossed in jail" (Genesis 40:14–15, Luke 23:42).

Joseph was never kidnapped. He did not tell the truth about what happened to him. I wonder if he did not want them to know his brothers were cruel to him and sold him off. It could be uncomfortable to talk to people about family problems. Siblings are supposed to love you, protect you, and give you support. Instead, Joseph's brothers tossed him out to the wolves.

When the chief cook observed what Joseph and the servant were talking about, he wanted to tell Joseph his dream to get its meaning. "So in my dream," the chief cook told Joseph, "I was carrying three bread baskets stacked on top of my head. The top basket was full of all kinds of baked things for the king, but birds were eating them" (Genesis 40:16–17).

Thus, Joseph said, "This is the meaning of your dream. The three baskets are three days, and in three days, the king will cut off your head. After that, he will hang your body on a pole, and birds will come and peck at it" (Genesis 40:18–19).

Three days later, it was the king's birthday, and he had dinner served for his guest. The king requested for his servant and chief cook to come to the dinner party. Sadly, he told the servant he could have his job back and had the cook put to death (Genesis 40:20–22, Matthew 14:6, Mark 6:21). And everything Joseph told them would happen did. But the servant forgot to mention Joseph to the king (Genesis 40:23).

Joseph was seventeen when his brothers tossed him in the dry well. One year later, he ran from Potiphar's wife and was put in jail, making him eighteen. God was in control of Joseph's life, yet it was not his time to be released from prison. So I am going to close this letter. Until the following letter.

Love,
Grandma

Forty-First Chapter Letter

Joseph Interprets the King's Dreams

Hello, grandkids! It is May 26, 2021, and it's 6:47 p.m. I am so excited about finishing this book. Reading about Joseph's life is traumatic. Can you imagine getting dumped off somewhere at the age of seventeen and not knowing where you may end up? This type of situation happens with foster kids. Joseph must have been confused and heartbroken that his family abandoned him. But God had his back the entire time. He saw his father, Jacob, build altars, worship God, and walk by faith, so he too leaned on his faith. I work hard to walk by faith so that my sons and grandkids and great-grandkids can do the same. What are you doing to show your dedication to God in front of your family members?

The last letter shared how Joseph told the meaning of two individuals' dreams and asked one of the men to tell the king about him to get out of prison, which he forgot. In chapter 41 of Genesis, I will share how Joseph interpreted the king's dreams, and because of that, he was made governor over Egypt at thirty! This chapter is long. It has fifty-seven verses, but it gets interesting as the story unfolds.

Two years passed when the king of Egypt had a dream. "In his dream, he was standing by the Nile River" (Genesis 41:1). Suddenly, seven healthy, fat cows came from the river and started eating grass along the riverbank (Genesis 41:2). Soon after that, seven ugly skinny cows came out of the river and ate the healthy, fat cows. After his dream, he immediately woke up for a short moment (Genesis 41:3–

4), fell back to sleep, and had another dream. The king dreamed that seven full heads of grain were growing on a single stalk (Genesis 41:5). Shortly after, seven other heads of grain appeared. They were thin and scorched by the east wind (Genesis 41:6–7). The king woke up and realized he was dreaming.

The next day, the king thought about his dream and became upset. He wanted to know the meanings of his dreams and decided to ask his servants. He "called in his magicians and wise men and shared his dream with them, but none of them could tell him what the dream meant" (Genesis 41:8, Daniel 2:1, Matthew 2:1). Finally, the king's servant said, "Now I remember what I was supposed to tell you" (Genesis 41:9). The servant told the king his experiences in jail with Joseph. He said, "When you were mad and angry at the cook and me, you tossed us both in jail in the house of the captain of the guard. And one night, we both had dreams, and each dream had a different meaning" (Genesis 41:10–11). The servant explained to his king that a young Hebrew man who was a servant to the captain guard interpreted their dreams. And everything happened just like he said. Finally, the servant said, "I got my job back, and the cook was put to death" (Genesis 41:12–13).

After the king heard this servant's story, he sent for Joseph. Joseph was released from jail immediately. Then they made Joseph shave and put on clean clothes to see the king (Genesis 41:14, Psalm 105:20, Daniel 2:25). When the king met Joseph, he said, "I had a dream, and no one can explain what it means. However, I am told you can interpret dreams" (Genesis 41:15, Daniel 5:16).

Joseph replied, "Your Majesty, I cannot do it myself, but God can give meaning to your dreams" (Genesis 42:42).

Once again, Joseph gives God praises! When you can share God's blessings with others, please do not hesitate. Tell the world how God has worked in your life and blessed you! Share the good news. Joseph knew God gave him the power to interpret dreams, saving his life and making him wealthy.

The king shared the dream with Joseph. "I dreamed I was standing on the bank of the Nile River and saw seven fat, healthy cows come up out of the river and begin feeding on the grass" (Genesis

41:16–18, Daniel 2:30). Next, there were "seven skinny, bony cows who came up out of the river, and I have never seen such ugly-looking cows anywhere in Egypt. The skinny cows ate the fat ones, but it was hard to tell because the thin cows were just as thin as they were before. Right after that dream, I woke up" (Genesis 41:19-21).

The king said, "I also had a dream that I saw seven heads of grain growing on one stalk. The heads were full and ripe. Then seven other heads of grain came up. They were thin and scorched by a wind from the desert" (Genesis 41:22–23). He said, "The heads of grains swallowed the full ones." The king told Joseph that he told his magicians his dreams, but they could not tell him the meanings (Genesis 41:24, Isaiah 8:19). Joseph listened to the king and replied, "Your Majesty, both of the dreams mean the same thing, and in them, God has shown what he is going to do" (Genesis 42:25, Daniel 2:28–29).

> The seven cows stand for seven years, and so do the seven good heads of grain. The seven skinny, ugly cows that came up later also stand for seven years, as do the seven bad heads of grain scorched by the east wind. The dreams mean there will be seven years when there will not be enough food. (Genesis 42:26–27, 2 Kings 8:1)

Joseph said,

> It is just as I said, God has shown what he intends to do. For seven years, Egypt will have more than enough grain. But that will be followed by seven years when there will not be enough grain. The good years of plenty of grain will be forgotten, and people will be starving in Egypt. The famine will be so bad that no one will remember that once there had been plenty of grain. (Genesis 41:28–31)

Joseph just described how humans easily forget when they have been showered with blessings and goods. People tend not to save for a rainy day. It is about managing your profits and saving for a rainy day. There will be a financial hardship for some people, and God tells us we must save for dry seasons.

Joseph told the king that "God had given him two dreams to let him know that he must do something very soon." First, Joseph suggested to the king that he should find someone who could oversee Egypt's crops. "Find a person who is wise and will know what to do and put him in charge of all Egypt" (Genesis 41:32–33, Numbers 23:19). Second, Joseph told the king to appoint some officials to collect one-fifth of every crop harvested in Egypt during the seven years when there is plenty of grain and give them the power to manage the grain during those good years and store it in the cities (Genesis 41:34–35, Proverbs 6:6–8). Joseph said it should be kept until it is needed during the seven years when there will not be enough grain in Egypt. Doing this "will keep the country from being destroyed because of the lack of food" (Genesis 41:36).

So again, saving for tough seasons is wise, or if you have been blessed with overwhelming wealth, hire someone to help you manage your wealth, just like Joseph recommended the king to do with his wealth.

Joseph Is Made Governor over Egypt

The king and his officials were amazed at Joseph's ability to interpret dreams that he was convinced Joseph should be the one to oversee the crops in Egypt. The king said, "No one could handle this better than Joseph, since the Spirit of God is with him" (Genesis 41:37–38, Acts 7:10, Numbers 27:18). It is a powerful statement from the king. He knew God had Joseph's back and confirmed it in front of his officials. "The king told Joseph, 'God is the one who has shown you these things. No one else is as wise as you are or know what you know'" (Genesis 41:39). The king put Joseph in charge of the palace and everyone. The people in the castle would have to obey Joseph. No one would be overseeing Joseph but the king. The king made Joseph the governor of all Egypt (Genesis 41:40–41, Psalm 105:21, Daniel 6:3).

What a beautiful feeling Joseph must have felt after being abandoned by his family and imprisoned for twelve years although some may say thirteen years. He is finally appreciated and honored by the king because of his faith in God. Trusting and having faith in God will be a life-changing experience for anyone who believes, as Joseph did.

After the king announced Joseph's leadership role, he "took off his royal ring and put it on Joseph's finger. Then, he gave him fine clothing to wear and placed a gold chain around his neck" (Genesis 41:42, Esther 3:10). Next, the king let Joseph ride in a chariot next to his own, and people were shouting, "Make way for Joseph!" He was the new governor of Egypt (Genesis 41:43). Finally, the king told Joseph, "Although I am the king, no one in Egypt is to do anything without your permission." He gave Joseph the Egyptian name Zaphenath Paneah and let him marry Asenath, the daughter of Potiphera, a priest in the city of Heliopolis. After that, Joseph traveled all over Egypt (Genesis 41:44–45).

Joseph was thirty years old when the king made him governor, and he went everywhere for the king. So for seven years, there were big harvests of grain (Genesis 41:46–47, 1 Samuel 16:21). "Joseph collected and stored up the extra grain in the cities of Egypt near the field where it was harvested." Therefore, there was so much grain they stopped keeping a record because it counted like the grains of sand along the beach (Genesis 41:48–49).

Joseph and his wife had two sons before the famine began. "Their first son was named Manasseh, which means God has let me forget all my troubles and family back home" (Genesis 41:50–51, Psalm 45:10). Their second son was Ephraim, which means, "God has made me a success in the land where I suffered" (Genesis 41:52). Thus, Joseph was genuinely blessed.

We all experience some trauma in our lives, but we cannot hold on to the past pain and hurt because it will affect our relationships with others. Seek God and keep him close and do not give up on faith. God will see you through your pain as he did with Joseph.

Egypt's seven years of having plenty of grain came to an end. "The seven years of famine began, just like Joseph predicted" (Genesis 41:53–54, Acts 7:11). There was not enough food in other countries, but there was plenty of food all over Egypt. "When the famine finally struck Egypt, the people asked the king for food, but he said, 'Go to Joseph and do what he tells you to do'" (Genesis 41:55, John 2:5). "The famine became bad everywhere in Egypt, so Joseph opened the storehouses and sold the grain to the Egyptians. People world-wide came to Egypt because the famine was severe in their countries" (Genesis 41:56–57, Ezekiel 29:12).

The famine in the countries resulted in a shortage of grain and food for seven years. However, God blessed Joseph with the knowledge to interpret dreams that told him the future, and because of that, Joseph saved people's lives. There was enough food for everyone who asked or purchased it from Joseph. The love our Lord Jesus Christ has for us and the people in this story is phenomenal. God chose and used Joseph to save people in Egypt and around the other counties from the famine. God knows what is going to happen in our lives and future. Keep God close to your heart and mind. Stay in prayer because he knows your pain. I cannot say it enough to trust God with all your hearts and not lean on your understanding (Proverbs 3:5–6). He is real! I am going to close this letter. Until the next time.

Love,
Grandma

Forty-Second Chapter Letter

Joseph's Brothers Go to Egypt to Buy Grain

Good morning, grandkids. I hope you have been taking care of yourselves and staying in prayer. Today is June 3, 2021, and it is 9:00 a.m. I have been helping your cousin Natalie move into her new home this week. She will be renting Grandma Josie's townhouse. The long-term plan will be for us to buy the unit if it is in God's will. Today is 123 days that I have been caring for Grandma Josie. Her dementia continues to take her memory, although she is healthy physically, thank the Lord.

In the last letter, I shared how Joseph interpreted the king's dreams, and because of that, the king made him governor over Egypt at thirty years old. In this letter, I will talk about Joseph's brothers visiting Egypt to buy grain. The brothers finally saw their Joseph after twenty-two years, but they did not know the governor was their brother. Therefore, Joseph did not reveal who he was in this forty-second chapter of Genesis.

When Joseph's father, Jacob, heard that there was grain in Egypt, he told his sons, "Why are you just sitting here, staring at one another? I have found out there is grain in Egypt. Go down and buy some so we will not starve to death" (Genesis 42:1–2, Acts 7:12). Therefore, Jacob sent ten of his sons to Egypt to buy grain. Jacob, however, did not send his younger son, Benjamin, with them. He was afraid that something might happen to him (Genesis 42:3–4). Thus, Jacob's sons joined others from Canaan who went to Egypt because of grain shortage (Genesis 42:5, Acts 7:11).

Joseph was the governor of Egypt and was in control of selling the grain. When his brothers came to see him and bowed their faces to the ground, they did not recognize Joseph (Genesis 42:6). Joseph knew right away that these men were his brothers standing in front of him, wanting to buy grain. As a result, he pretended not to know them and spoke to them harshly and asked, "Where do you come from?" They replied, "From the land of Canaan, we have come to buy grain" (Genesis 42:7–8).

Joseph remembered his dream about his brothers. Therefore, he said, "You are spies! You have come to our country to see if we are weak" (Genesis 42:9).

They said, "No, sir! We are your servants, and we have come to buy grain. We are honest men and come from the same family. Thus, we are not spies" (Genesis 42:10–11). Joseph insisted that they were spies, and his brothers tried telling him they were not.

Finally, Joseph said, "You have come here to find out if our country is weak" (Genesis 42:12).

The brothers said, "Sir, we come from a family of twelve brothers. The youngest is with our father in Canaan, and our other brother is dead" (Genesis 42:13).

Joseph said, "It is just like I said. You are spies, and I will find out who you are, and I swear by the life of the king that you will not leave this place until your youngest brother comes here" (Genesis 42:14–15, 1 Samuel 1:26). Consequently, Joseph told his brothers, "One of you get your youngest brother, and the rest of you stay here in jail. This way, I will know whether you guys are telling the truth. But if you guys are lying, I swear by the king that you are spies" (Genesis 42:16).

Joseph wanted desperately to see his younger brother, Benjamin, so he threatened his brothers. Joseph continued to act like he did not know who these men were.

Joseph kept them in jail for three days before he said to them, "Since I respect God, I will give you a chance to save your lives. If you guys are sincere men, one of you stay here in jail, and the rest of you can take the gain to your starving family" (Genesis 42:17–19, Leviticus 25:43). Joseph told his brothers to bring back their little brother to him. He promised them that they would not be put to death if they told the truth, and the brothers agreed (Genesis 42:20).

When the brothers were in jail, they talked among themselves and reflected on how they treated their little brother Joseph. Finally, they said to each other, "We are being punished because of the way we treated Joseph. We saw the trouble he was in, but we refused to help him when he begged us." Thus, the brothers felt they were serving their consequences (Genesis 42:21, Hosea 5:15, Proverbs 21:13, Matthew 7:2). Nevertheless, the oldest brother, Reuben, spoke up and said, "I told you not to harm the boy." Again they felt they were paying for their mistake, for killing him (Genesis 42:22, 2 Chronicles 24:22, Psalm 9:12). But Joseph never died. God was using him to help others during these crises. While they were talking, Joseph was listening, and he understood what they were saying. But they did not know Joseph knew what they were saying because he was speaking through an interpreter (Genesis 42:23).

It hurt Joseph listening to his brothers talking about how they oppressed him and tossed him into the dry well. So Joseph turned away from them and started crying. He did not want them to see him emotional. Shortly after, Joseph returned and spoke to them again. He had his brother Simeon tied up and taken away while the other brothers watched (Genesis 42:24).

Joseph's Brothers Return to Canaan

Joseph gave orders to his servants to fill his brothers' sacks with grain and put their money back in their sacks. He also told his servants to make sure they had enough food for their travel back home. Once this happened, the brothers each loaded up their donkeys and left (Genesis 42:25–26, Romans 12:17, Matthew 5:44, 1 Peter 3:9).

When the brothers were traveling back home and were tired, they stopped to rest for the night, and one of them opened his grain bag to feed his donkey and immediately saw his money bag. He

DR. SYLVIA GALVEZ

could not believe his eyes. Therefore, he told his brothers, "Here is my money, in my bag."

They all stopped and stared at each other with fear and said, "What has God done to us" (Genesis 42:27–28)? When they returned to their hometown Canaan, they told their father Jacob everything that had happened to them. They said, "The governor of Egypt was rude and treated us like spies" (Genesis 42:29–30). They explained to their father, Jacob, that they had to convince the governor that they were "honest men, not spies" and "we come from a family of twelve brothers" with the youngest at home with his dad and another one dead (Genesis 42:31–32). Jacob listened to his sons while they were sharing their experiences.

The sons told their father that the governor told them the only way he could find out the truth if they were honest people was they would have to leave one of the brothers in jail while they brought home the grain to their starving families and that they must bring the youngest brother back to Egypt to prove that they were honest people and not spies (Genesis 42:33–34). The governor said, after that, he would let their brother out of jail, and they could stay there and trade goods (Genesis 42:35).

Jacob did not understand why this was happening to his family. Finally, the sons told Jacob, their father, that they found their money bags in the grain when they emptied their grain sacks. They were all afraid, and so was their father, Jacob. Jacob said, "You have already taken my sons Joseph and Simeon from me. And now you want to take away Benjamin! Everything is against me."

The oldest son, Reuben, spoke up, "Father, if I do not bring Benjamin back home, you can kill both of my sons. Trust me with him, I will bring him back" (Genesis 42:36–37).

Jacob said, "I will not let my son Benjamin go down to Egypt with the rest of you. His brother is already dead, and he is my only son left. I am an old man, and if anything happens to him on the way to Egypt, I will die from sorrow, and all of you will be to blame" (Genesis 42:38).

Jacob loved Joseph and Benjamin more than his other sons because they were from Rachel, whom he loved more than anything.

The brothers said, "We are being punished because of the way we treated Joseph." They knew one day they would have to pay for their sins because of what they did to Joseph 13 years ago. Sins are always revealed. God sees everything! Until the following letter.

Love,
Grandma

Forty-Third Chapter Letter

Joseph's Brothers Return to Egypt with Benjamin

Good evening, my grandkids. I hope you are doing well and enjoying the letters. Today is June 4, 2021, and it is 8:00 p.m.

In the last letter, I shared how Joseph's ten brothers went to Egypt to buy grain, and they had to communicate with the governor to purchase more. The governor was their brother Joseph. They did not know Joseph was the governor, but Joseph knew who his brothers were and pretended he did not know them. Therefore, Joseph accused his brothers of being spies. But Joseph knew they were not spying; he just wanted to see his little brother. So they were ordered to bring back their little brother, Benjamin, so the governor could see him and to verify they were not spying and were honest men. In this next chapter, Genesis 34, I will discuss the brothers bringing Benjamin to Egypt to meet the governor, and they all had dinner together at Joseph's home.

Time had passed by, and Jacob did not send his sons back to Egypt right away with Benjamin as requested by the governor. Instead, it was not until the famine in Canaan had gotten so bad Jacob started running out of food. Jacob and his family had eaten all the grain they purchased from Egypt, so Jacob told his sons, "Go back and buy some more grain" (Genesis 43:1–2).

His son Judah said, "The governor strictly warned us that we would not be allowed to see him unless we brought our younger brother Benjamin along to meet him. We will then be allowed to buy more grain, and our brother Simeon will be released from jail." Judah told his father, Jacob, he could not go back to Egypt until he allowed Benjamin to come with them (Genesis 43:3–5). They refused to go without their younger brother, Benjamin.

Jacob was so afraid to let Benjamin go. Finally, he told his sons, "Why did you cause me so much trouble by telling the governor you had another brother" (Genesis 43:6)?

His sons said, "The governor asked us a lot of questions about our family. He even wanted to know if you were still alive and if we had other brothers." The sons told their father that all they did was answer all the questions the governor was asking. And they did not know that the governor was going to ask to bring their little brother to Egypt (Genesis 43:7).

Judah tried convincing his father, Jacob. He said, "Let Benjamin go with me, and we will leave right away so that no one will starve to death." Judah promised his father he would bring Benjamin back to safety, and if he did not, he could blame him for the rest of his life. However, his sons felt that their father, Jacob, allowed too much time to pass by, not allowing them to go back to Egypt right away. Judah said, "If we had not wasted all this time, we could have been there and back twice" (Genesis 43:8–10, Philemon 1:18–19).

Jacob finally agreed and said, "If you take Benjamin, take the governor a gift of the best things from our country, for example, perfume, honey, spices, pistachio nuts, and almonds." They also took twice the amount of money for the grain because they felt there must have been a mistake when they found the money in their grain sacks (Genesis 43:11–12, Proverbs 18:16, Ezekiel 27:17). Jacob told his sons to take Benjamin and leave right away (Genesis 34:13).

Jacob told his sons, when they see the governor, "I pray that God All-Powerful will be good to you and that the governor will let your other brother and Benjamin come back home with you. I hope I do not lose my children, but I guess it was meant to be if I do" (Genesis 43:14, Esther 4:16). So the sons packed up and left right away with Benjamin. They took gifts, twice the amount of money Jacob told them to take, and they traveled to Egypt (Genesis 43:15).

When they arrived in Egypt, they faced the governor, their brother Joseph. They stood in from of him with Benjamin next to them. When Joseph saw his little brother, he immediately asked his servants in charge of his house to "take these men to my home and slaughter an animal and cook it so they can have lunch with me." So the servant did what Joseph wanted and took the men to his house.

The brothers did not understand what was going on. They were afraid and said to themselves, "We are being taken to his home because of the money that was put back in our sacks last time. He will arrest us, make us his servants, and take our donkeys" (Genesis 43:16–18). Joseph's brothers were worried about their lives. They did not know what to expect.

When they arrived at Joseph's home, they started talking to the servant in charge because they were concerned about their safety (Genesis 43:19). The brothers told the servant, "Sir, we came to Egypt once before to buy grain, but when we stopped for the night, we each found the sack money we paid for the grain, the exact amount we had paid, and we brought extra money with us to buy more grain" (Genesis 43:20–22).

The servant said it was all right. "Do not worry. The God you and your father worship must have put the money there because I received your payment in full." The servant then released their brother Simeon out of jail and escorted him to Joseph's house (Genesis 43:23).

The servant in charge of Joseph's house took the brothers into the home and gave them water to wash their feet. He also cared for their donkeys (Genesis 43:24). After that, the brothers got the gifts ready to give to their brother Joseph since they overheard they were going to have lunch with the governor in his home (Genesis 43:25). When Joseph entered the room, they gave him the gifts they had brought and bowed their faces down. Then Joseph asked them how they were doing and about their elderly father. He wondered if Jacob was still alive and asked if he was still living. They answered, "Your servant, our father, is still alive and well." Then they bowed their heads down again to Joseph (Genesis 43:26–28).

Joseph looked around and saw his little brother, Benjamin. "This must be your little brother, the one you told me about." Joseph then said, "God bless you, my son." Joseph was so emotional after seeing his brother he immediately turned away into another room and cried because of the love he had for his little brother, Benjamin (Genesis 43:29–30). Then he washed his face before he went back out to face his brothers. After that, Joseph was able to control his emotions.

Joseph told his servants to "serve the meal!" Joseph sat at a table by himself, and his brothers were at another table. And the Egyptians also sat at another table because they did not like sitting with Hebrews. It was disgusting to them (Genesis 43:31–32). Joseph's brothers were honored to be eating with the governor at his house. They were seated in front of Joseph according to their ages, from the oldest to the youngest (Genesis 43:33). The food was on Joseph's table. The brothers were served food from Joseph's table, and Benjamin was given five times more food than his other brothers. Joseph had a fantastic time eating and drinking with his brothers, and they did not even know the governor was their brother.

Finally, Jacob let go and trusted God because he said, "I pray that God All-Powerful will be good to you and the governor will let your brother and Benjamin come back home" (Genesis 43:14). Joseph's servant in charge told the brothers "do not worry" about the money in their grain sack because the God that their father worshipped must have put the money in their bag because they were paid in full for the gain (Genesis 43:23).

Joseph had this situation all planned out. He loved his brothers regardless of what he went through in the past twenty-two years. He was happy to see them. He knew God was in control of his life and did not worry about the future. But on the other hand, his brothers did not understand why they were getting treated remarkably by the governor. They did not know their brother Joseph was behind the scenes. We never know what God has in store for us. Our job is to trust him. Until the following letter.

Love,
Grandma

Forty-Fourth Chapter Letter

Joseph Planted His Silver
Cup in the Grain Sack

Dear, grandkids, how are you doing? Today is Sunday, June 6, 2021. It is 1:44 p.m. In the last letter, I wrote about Joseph's brothers returning to Egypt with their little brother, Benjamin, as the governor requested. When the brothers arrived in Egypt with Benjamin, the governor invited them to have lunch in his home with him. So they all sat at a different table, with Joseph sitting in front of them. The brothers sat according to their ages, from the oldest to the youngest. In this letter, I will discuss the brothers leaving Egypt after spending time with the governor, their brother, and buying grain. Joseph had his servant in charge put his silver cup in his little brother Benjamin's grain sack on purpose.

After lunch with the governor, he told his servant to fill the brothers' grain sacks with as much as possible and put the money back in the bags. He also requested his servant to put his silver cup in the youngest brother's sack (Genesis 44:1–2). Early the following day, the brothers were on their way home with their donkeys. They were not too far off from the city when Joseph told his servant to "go after those men! And when you catch up to them say, 'My master has been good to you, so why have you stolen his silver cup?' Let them know that I drink from that cup and use it to learn about the future and that they have done a terrible thing" (Genesis 44:3–5, 1 Samuel

25:21). Joseph was doing anything he could to bring his little brother Benjamin back. He wanted his family but was not ready to reveal who he was yet.

When the servant caught up with the brothers, he did what the governor ordered him to say. The brothers could not believe what they were hearing and said, "Sir, why do you say such a thing? We would never do such a thing like that! We even brought back the money we found in our grain sacks when we were in Canaan. So why would we want to steal any silver or gold from your master's house?" The brothers told the servant if he found the cup on any of them, he could kill him, and the rest of them could be their servants (Genesis 44:6–9).

The servant said, "Okay, good! I will do what you say. Thus, whoever has the cup will become my servant, and the rest of you can go free" (Genesis 44:10).

The brothers immediately removed their sack from the ground and opened it (Genesis 44:11).

Joseph's servant started searching the oldest brother's sack first and went to the others, and when he came to the youngest brother's sack, Benjamin's, he found the cup (Genesis 44:12). The brother could not believe what they saw and was mad and started crying, tearing off their clothes in sorrow. Finally, they loaded up their donkeys and went back to Egypt to talk to Joseph (Genesis 44:13, 2 Samuel 1:11). When Judah and his brothers arrived, they saw Joseph was still in his home, so they went to Joseph and bowed down.

Joseph said, "What have you done? Shouldn't you have known I could find out?" (Genesis 44:14–15).

Judah said, "Sir, what can we say? How can we prove we are innocent?" Judah believed that God has shown that they were guilty and knew they would become servants, and for sure, Benjamin, who had the cup in his bag (Genesis 44:16).

Joseph listened and said, "I would never punish all of you. Only the one who was caught with the cup will become my servant, and the rest of you can go back to your father" (Genesis 44:17, Proverbs 17:15). Nevertheless, the brothers felt helpless because they were faced with a problem they could not get out of. Reuben promised

Jacob, his father, to bring Benjamin back home safe, but the situation was out of his hands.

Judah Pleads for Benjamin's Freedom

The brothers felt powerless about Benjamin becoming a servant to the governor. So Judah stepped up and went to Joseph and said, "Sir, you have as much power as the king himself, and I am your servant, but please do not get mad if I speak" (Genesis 44:18, Proverbs 17:15). Therefore, Judah told the governor, "You asked us questions, and we told you the truth. You asked if our father was still alive and if we had any more brothers, and we told you, 'Our father is a very old man, and that Benjamin was born when our father was old in age, and his other brother was dead.' Benjamin is the only one of the two brothers who are still alive, and our father loves him very much" (Genesis 44:18–20, Exodus 32:22). Judah continued explaining how the governor ordered them to bring Benjamin back to Egypt to see him, and they did. They told the governor their father would die if Benjamin would not come back with them (Genesis 44:21–22).

Judah said, "Governor, you warned us that we could not see you unless we brought our little brother back to Egypt to see you, so we told our father what you said" (Genesis 44:23–24). He explained to the governor that their father, Jacob, agreed to have them come back and buy more grain, but they had to convince their father to bring Benjamin with them. Finally, Judah said, "I told my father that we could not go back to Egypt without our younger brother because we would not be able to see the governor" (Genesis 44:25–26). Judah told the governor that his father, Jacob, reminded him that his favorite wife was Rachel and that she gave him two sons, and one was already missing for a long time and that he thinks he was torn to pieces by some wild animal (Genesis 44:27–28).

Judah pleaded with the governor by telling him they must take Benjamin back to their father because Jacob told his sons, "I am an old man. If you take Benjamin from me and something happens to him, I will die of a broken heart" (Genesis 44:29). Nevertheless, Judah carried on with why it was urgent to take Benjamin home. He said, "Benjamin must be with us when I go back to my father. Our father loves him so much, if Benjamin does not come back with me, that will kill him. And I promised my father that I would bring him home safe, and If I did not, he could blame me for the rest of my life" (Genesis 44:30–32, 1 Samuel 18:1). So he begged the governor by saying, "Sir, I am your servant. Please let me stay here in place of Benjamin and let him return home with his brothers. I will not be able to face my father if Benjamin is not with me. I cannot bear to see my father in sorrow" (Genesis 44:33–34, Exodus 32:32).

Judah was not the oldest son but stepped up, took the leadership role, and agreed to be the governor's servant instead of his younger brother Benjamin. I am sure all eleven of the brothers remembered seeing their father's pain when Joseph never came home. Judah and his brothers did not want to walk away and make the same mistake they did with their brother Joseph. However, Joseph listened to his brother plead for Benjamin, and it hurt him. He loved all his brothers no matter how they treated him in the past. Therefore, Joseph did not want to hold on to any grudges or resentment. But he did watch them plead for a while for their little brother's life.

Are you holding on to any past hurt and pain from your siblings, friends, or parents? Are you ready to let go of the pain and face the person? I am going to close this letter. Until the following one.

Love, Grandma

Forty-Fifth Chapter Letter

Joseph Tells His Brothers Who He Is

Good evening, grandkids! It is Sunday, June 6, 2021. It is 7:40 p.m. I finished the last letter early today and wanted to pick up where I left off. In the previous letter, I shared how Governor Joseph planted his silver cup in his younger brother Benjamin's grain sack on purpose to get him to stay in Egypt. However, his older brothers refused to let that happen and pleaded with the governor to take Benjamin home and not make him a servant. In this letter, I will share what happens in Genesis, chapter 45. Joseph finally told his brothers who he was, and they became emotional. Then Joseph invited his entire family to move to Egypt with him, including his father, Jacob, because a five-year famine would still occur.

Joseph listened to his brothers plead for Benjamin to return home with them. Thus, Joseph could not continue to hold his feelings in front of his brothers anymore and excused his servants by making them leave the room. When the servants left the room, and he was alone with his brothers, he told them, "I am Joseph." Then he cried loudly, and the Egyptians overheard him and immediately informed the officials in the king's palace (Genesis 45:1–2, Acts 7:13). His brothers did not believe him at the beginning. Joseph asked his brothers if their father was still alive, but they were too frightened to answer because they did not believe him. Finally, Joseph told his brothers to "come closer to him, and they did" (Genesis 45:3).

Joseph was relieved and happy his brothers knew the truth about who he was. Joseph said, "Yes, I am your brother Joseph, the one you sold into Egypt (Genesis 45:4). Joseph told his brother not to worry or blame themselves for what they did because he felt God is the one who sent him ahead to save lives. He explained to his brothers that there had been a famine for two years already, and for the next five years, no one will be able to plow the fields or harvest grain (Genesis 45:6). Therefore, "God sent me on ahead of you to keep your families alive and to save you in this beautiful way" (Genesis 45:7).

Most importantly, Joseph believed God sent him to Egypt to help people. He said, "It was God. He made me the highest official in the king's court and placed me over all Egypt" (Genesis 45:8, Romans 8:28). Furthermore, Joseph told his brothers to hurry home and tell their father that "God has made him ruler of Egypt" and to hurry back (Genesis 45:9).

Joseph was so excited that he informed his brothers that they could live near him in the region of Goshen with their children and grandchildren, along with their sheep, goats, cattle, and everything they owned. He said, "I will take care of you there during the next five years of famine, but if you do not come back, you and your family and animals will starve to death" (Genesis 45:11). The brothers listened to Joseph with disbelief. They were shocked! Joseph again tried to prove to his brothers who he was. "All of you, including my brother Benjamin, could tell by what I have said that I am Joseph." Then he told them to tell their father about his great power in Egypt and about everything they have witnessed. Joseph wanted his father to come and see for himself. Thus, he told them to hurry and bring their father to Egypt (Genesis 45:12–13, Acts 7:14).

Joseph and Benjamin hugged each other and started crying. Joseph cried as he kissed each of his brothers, and then they believed him and started talking to him (Genesis 45:14–15). When the king and his official heard that Joseph's brothers were in his home, they were happy for Joseph.

The king said to Joseph, "Tell your brothers to load their donkeys and return to Canaan. Have them bring their father and their families here. I will give them the best land in Egypt, and they can eat and enjoy everything that grows on it" (Genesis 45:16–18). The king was overjoyed for Joseph. He said, "Joseph, make sure your brothers take some wagons from Egypt for their wives and children to ride in. In addition, make sure they bring their father and to leave their possessions behind because they will be given the best of everything in Egypt" (Genesis 45:19–20).

The brothers agreed to do what the king said. Therefore, Joseph gave them wagons and food for their trip home like the king instructed (Genesis 45:21). Benjamin received five new outfits and three hundred pieces of silver (Genesis 45:22, 2 Kings 5:5). Joseph gave his brothers ten donkeys loaded with the best things in Egypt and ten other donkeys loaded with grain and bread and other foods for their return trip. Joseph instructed the brothers, "Do not argue on your way home" (Genesis 45:23–24)!

The brothers left Egypt, and when they arrived in Canaan, they told their father, Jacob, Joseph was still alive and was the ruler of Egypt. Their father could not believe what he was hearing and was surprised (Genesis 45:26, Job 29:24). Then they told him everything Joseph had said. Then when Jacob saw the wagons Joseph had sent, his father felt better (Genesis 45:27). So Jacob said, "Now I can believe you! My son Joseph must be alive, and I will get to see him before I die" (Genesis 45:28).

The brothers could not believe what was happening when Joseph revealed himself to them. Joseph was emotionally over-whelmed, cried and cried while he kissed his brothers one by one. The brothers were speechless and afraid. Joseph did not blame them for tossing him in the well. Instead, he said, "God sent him ahead to save lives." It was God who made him ruler over Egypt! Joseph was proud of how God used him in this situation. He was kind and generous to his brothers and happy to share his goods and home environment. Joseph never brought up the pain and hurt his brother caused him those twenty-two years. Instead, he felt blessed that God used him to save people from starvation and death.

God is real! And he will come through on his timing. It is not our time but God's timing in our lives that matters. Therefore, we must not give up, stay in prayer, be patient, and wait for the Lord.

Joseph had to wait a long time but did not become bitter. He waited because he knew the God his forefather served and worshiped had his back! Do you trust and believe God has your back? Has God used you in a situation you were not happy with at the time, but in the end, you realized and learned God put you in that position for a reason? What a beautiful ending. Jacob's family reunited after being separated for twenty-two years. It is never too late to have hope and pray for family members who refuse to be a part of the entire family. Peace and until the next time.

Love,
Grandma

Forty-Sixth Chapter Letter

Jacob and His Family Move to Egypt

Good afternoon, my sweet grandkids. I hope you are doing well and staying in prayer. Today is Monday, June 7, 2021. It is 12:30 p.m.

In the last letter, I shared how Joseph revealed himself to his brothers. He could not hold his feelings back when Judah tried to convince him to let Benjamin go home with them. Joseph was very emotional and kissed all his brothers. He instructed his brothers to tell their father about Joseph's leadership role in Egypt. The king was happy for Joseph and his family. He invited them to live in the best part of Egypt and promised to give them the best of everything. In this letter, I will write what happened in Genesis, chapter 46. Jacob and his family moved to Egypt. On his way there, Jacob stopped at a town called Beersheba to worship God and thank him for everything, and God spoke to him. The story ends with a list of all Jacob's sons and their descendants. Jacob had a total of seventy family members move to Egypt.

After Jacob's sons told their father about Joseph, and he saw the wagons, he believed them. So Jacob packed up everything he owned and left for Egypt. On his way there, he stopped near the town of Beersheba and offered sacrifices to the God his father, Isaac, had worshiped. That night, God spoke to Jacob and said, "Jacob! Jacob!" And Jacob replied, "Here I am" (Genesis 46:1–2). God said, "I am God, the same God your father worshiped. Thus, do not be afraid to go to Egypt. I will give you so many descendants that they will become a nation. I will go with you to Egypt, and later I will bring your descendants back here. And your son Joseph will be at your side when you die" (Genesis 46:3–4).

Jacob and his family traveled from Beersheba and headed toward Egypt. His sons put their father in the wagon as the king instructed, and the small children and the wives were in the other wagons. Jacob's entire family traveled to Egypt, including his sons, grandsons, daughters, and granddaughters. They had all their animals and everything they owned (Genesis 46:5–7, Acts 7:15, Deuteronomy 26:5). When Jacob went to Egypt, his children, born in northern Syria, went along with their families. Below you will find the list of Jacob and his descendants that traveled to Egypt with him (Genesis 46:8).

Reuben was the firstborn of Jacob. The sons of Reuben: Hanoch, Pallu, Hezron, and Carmi (Genesis 46:9). Leah was his mother.

Simeon was the second born of Jacob. The sons of Simeon: Jemuel, Jamin, Ohad, Jakin, Zohar, and Shaul, the son of the Canaanite woman (Genesis 46:10). Leah was his mother.

Levi was the third born of Jacob. The sons of Levi: Gershon, Kohath, and Merari (Genesis 46:11). Leah was his mother.

Judah was the fourth born of Jacob. The sons of Judah: Er, Onan, Shelah, Perez, and Zerah (but Er and Onan died in the land of Canaan; Genesis 46:12). Leah was his mother.

Issachar was the fifth born of Leah and Jacob. The sons of Issachar: Tola, Puah, Jashub, and Shimron (Genesis 46:13). Leah was his mother.

Zebulum was the sixth born of Leah and Jacob. The sons of Zebulum: Sered, Elon, and Jahleel (Genesis 46:14). Leah was his mother.

These sons were of Leah, born to Jacob in Paddan Aram. They had a daughter named Dinah. There was a total of thirty-three (Genesis 46:15).

Leah's servant, Zilpah, had two sons born to Jacob, Gad and Asher.

Gad was born to Jacob. The sons of Gad: Zephon, Haggi, Shuni, Ezbon, Eri, Arodi, and Areli (Genesis 46:16). Their mother was Leah's servant, Zilpah.

Asher was born to Jacob. The sons of Asher: Imnah, Ishvah, and Beriah. They had a sister named Serah (Genesis 46:17).

Their mother was Leah's servant, Zilpah. Beriah had two sons, Heber and Malkiel.

These children were born to Jacob by Zilpah, Leah's servant. They had sixteen in total (Genesis 46:18).

The sons of Rachel, Jacob's wife had two sons named Joseph and Benjamin (Genesis 46:19). Manasseh and Ephraim were born to Joseph and his wife, Asenath, daughter of Potiphera, the priest of Heliopolis, in Egypt (Genesis 46:20).

The sons of Benjamin: Bela, Beker, Ashbel, Gera, Naaman, Ehi, Rosh, Muppim, Huppim, and Ard (Genesis 46:21).

There were fourteen sons born to Jacob and Rachel (Genesis 46:22).

Her servant Bilhah had two sons named Dan and Naphtali.

The son of Dan is named Hushim (Genesis 46:23).

The sons of Naphtali: Jahziel, Guni, Jezer, and Shillem (Genesis 46:24). "These were the sons born to Jacob by Bilhah, a servant given to Rachel by her father, Laban." They had seven children (Genesis 46:25).

Thus, sixty-six family members from Jacob went to Egypt, not including his daughter-in-law (Genesis 46:26). Jacob's two grandsons, born in Egypt, made a total of seventy members of Jacob's family in Egypt (Genesis 46:27).

While Jacob was traveling toward Egypt, he asked his son Judah to go ahead and ask his son Joseph to meet him in Goshen (Genesis 46:28). Shortly after, Joseph got into his chariot and went to meet his father. When they saw each other, Joseph hugged his father and cried for a long time. Finally, Jacob told Joseph, "Now that I have seen you and know you are still alive, I am ready to die" (Genesis 46:29–30, Luke 2:29–30).

Joseph told his family that he must report to the king that his family had arrived from Canaan (Genesis 46:31). Joseph said, "I will tell the king that you are shepherds and that you have brought your sheep, goats, cattle, and everything you own" (Genesis 46:32). Joseph was giving his brothers a heads up about the king's likes and dislikes regarding flocks. He said, "The king will call you in and ask what you do for a living. Please make sure when you see him say, 'We are shepherds. And our families have always raised sheep.' If you say this, the king will let you settle in the region of Goshen." Joseph wanted his family to say they raised sheep to the king because Egyptians do not like to be around people who raised sheep (Genesis 46:33–34).

Jacob felt blessed because of how Joseph's life turned out. He wanted to express his thanks to God by stopping by Beersheba and offer sacrifices to the God of his father, Isaac. Jacob's father, Isaac, and grandfather Abraham also stopped at Beersheba and offered sacrifices when they wanted to thank God. He knew it was God who watched over Joseph during those twenty-two years. How often do you thank God for your blessings? And do you have a special place where you spend time with God?

God said, "Jacob! Jacob! I am the same God your father worshiped, and do not be afraid. Go to Egypt, and I will be with you, and later you will have many descendants." Therefore, Jacob continued to walk by faith and went to Egypt. It is getting late, and I am going to close this letter. Until the following letter.

Love, Grandma

Forty-Seventh Chapter Letter

Joseph Introduced His Family to the King

Good morning, grandkids. Today is June 8, 2021, and it's 9:55 a.m. Grandma Josie and I are doing well. It has been 128 days since I have been caring for her. I hope you are doing well and keeping God first when making decisions.

In the last letter, I shared how Joseph invited his brothers, father, and the entire family to live in Egypt. I listed seventy of their family members who entered Egypt. And a side note, the name Perez is listed as one of Judah's sons, and Jesus came from that family line. Perez is Grandma Josie's family roots. Nevertheless, Jacob visited a town called Beersheba to offer sacrifices to God. In turn, God spoke to Jacob and reminded him he had his back and will have many descendants and not to be afraid to move to Egypt because he would be with him. Jacob and Joseph eventually meet and embrace each other.

In this letter, I will share with you what happened in Genesis, chapter 47. Joseph introduced his family to the king, and while they were living in Egypt, the fifth year of famine was happening. So the king allowed Jacob and his family to settle in Goshen, the northeastern part of Egypt.

When the family arrived in Egypt, Joseph asked five of his brothers to come with him to meet the king. Joseph said to the king,

"My father and brothers have come from Canaan, and they have brought their sheep, goats, cattle, and everything they owned to the region of Goshen." Then he introduced his brothers to the king.

The king said, "What do you do for a living?" The brothers replied, "Sir, we are shepherds. Our families have always raised sheep" (Genesis 47:1–3, Acts: 7:13).

Joseph's brother shared with the king that in Canaan, all the pastures have dried up, and their sheep had no grass to eat and if it was okay for them to live in the region of Goshen (Genesis 47:4). Thus, the king turned to Joseph and said, "It is good your father and brothers have arrived here. I will let them live anywhere they choose in the land of Egypt, but I suggest they settle in Goshen, which is the best part of our land. And I would like for your finest shepherds to oversee my sheep and goats" (Genesis 47:5–6). Shortly after, Joseph brought in his father, Jacob, to meet the king. And Jacob gave the king his blessings. Then the king said, "How old are you?" Jacob replied, "I have lived to be 130 and moved from place to place. My parents and grandparents have also had to move from place to place. They lived long lives but did not have a hard life as I have" (Genesis 47:7–9, Hebrews 11:9, Job 14:11). Jacob then gave the king his blessings again and left. Joseph obeyed the king and gave his father and brothers some of the best lands in Egypt near the city of Rameses. Joseph also gave them food for the family (Genesis 47:10–12, Exodus 1:11).

A Famine in Egypt

The famine Joseph predicted in the king's dream was happening everywhere in Egypt and Canaan. People were suffering and wanting to buy grain. So Joseph started selling the grain he had stored up and put the money in the king's treasury (Genesis 47:13–14). The people then started running out of money to buy grain. The Egyptians came to Joseph and demanded that he gave them grain. They said, "Give us more grain! If you do not, we will soon die because our money was depleted to buy grain" (Genesis 47:15).

Joseph replied, "If you do not have any more money, then give me your animals, and I will give you some grain." From that point on, the people started to bring Joseph their horses, donkeys, sheep, and goats in exchange for grain. And within that year, Joseph collected every animal in Egypt (Genesis 47:16–17).

The people approached Joseph again and said, "Sir, there is no way we can continue to hide the truth from you. We are broke and do not have any more animals to give for grain. We have nothing but ourselves and our land" (Genesis 47:18). The people told Joseph that they did not want to starve and let their land be ruined. They requested Joseph to give them grain to eat and seeds to plant, and in return, they would become the king's servants and sell him their land (Genesis 47:19). The famine was so severe that Joseph purchased every piece of land in Egypt for the king and made everyone the king's servants except the priests. The king gave the priests a food allowance so they did not have to sell their land (Genesis 47:20–22, Jeremiah 32:43, Ezra 7:24).

After Joseph agreed to help the people by giving them seeds for their land, he told them, "You and your land belong to the king" (Genesis 47:23). Joseph then explained that one-fifth of their crops would go to the king, and the rest of the seeds they could keep for food for the families (Genesis 47:24). The people were happy with that agreement and said, "Sir, you have saved our lives!" After that, they did not have any problems being the king's servants. From that point on, Joseph made a law that stated one-fifth of the harvest would always belong to the king. Thus the priests did not lose their land (Genesis 47:25–26).

I think some of us have experienced famine in our lives, a shortage of funds to buy food for the family or pay bills. A person can feel powerless having plenty for years, and then the resources end. So we must not take our situation for granted, our jobs or support system. Instead, save for future circumstances because we never know what lies ahead. But stay in prayer, and trust God will let you know what to expect as he did with Joseph.

Jacob Becomes an Old Man

"The people of Israel made their home in the land of Goshen, where they became prosperous and had large families. Jacob himself lived there for 17 years before dying at 147 years old" (Genesis 47:27–28). "Jacob knew he did not have long to live and called for Joseph to come and see him." Jacob told his son, Joseph, "If you love me, you must make a promise not to bury me in Egypt" (Genesis 47:29, Deuteronomy 31:14). "Instead, bury me in the place where my ancestors are buried" (Genesis 47:30). Joseph told his father, Jacob, he would do whatever he asked. And Jacob said, "Will you give me your word?" Joseph replied, "Yes, I will." After their conversation, Jacob bowed his head down and prayed at the head of his bed (Genesis 47:30–31).

Jacob's family members were honored to be in the presence of the king. Moreover, they were humbled about the invitation from the king and their brother Joseph to allow them to live in Goshen. Jacob shared with the king how hard his life had been. First, he had to leave his parent's home because he thought his brother would kill him. Then recall how hard he had to work for his uncle Laban to marry Rachel. And the most significant heartbreak is when his wife Rachel died and when Joseph never came home.

Sometimes we must experience heartaches in life, and we do not understand why until the end. Then we realize it was for the better. Therefore, do not be discouraged when you are faced with problems and pain. Jesus's brother James said, "We are to rejoice when faced with trials and tribulations" (James 1:2). There are reasons behind trials and tribulations, and only God knows why. Our job is to trust the process because God has it all planned out.

Joseph, on the other hand, was chosen by God to save people's lives, their land, and manage the king's palace. Thus, Joseph oversaw the people and the king's wealth. God knew Joseph's leadership skills beforehand and knew he would be the right person to help the king in Egypt and his people. God knows us better than we know ourselves. Therefore, we must trust God and believe he is always holding our hands one step at a time. I am going to close this letter. Until the next time.

Love,
Grandma

Forty-Eighth Chapter Letter

Jacob Blesses Joseph's Two Sons

Good morning, grandkids. I hope you are doing well and following along with your Bibles. Today is Wednesday, June 9, 2021. It is 9:45 a.m. Grandma Josie's memory continues to get worse. From time to time, she will wander off across the street, looking through the neighbor's window, who happen to be my nieces. And when I tell her not to look through their window and come back home, she will say I cannot tell her what to do! So there are some challenging days.

In the last chapter, I shared how Joseph introduced his family to the king and settled in Goshen. Then I talked about the famine and how it was in the fifth year. Finally, Jacob met the king and told him how difficult his life had been. When Jacob was 147, during this point in his life, he was getting ready to die. In this letter, I will continue to talk about Jacob and how he blessed his son Joseph and his two sons.

When Joseph heard his father Jacob had become very ill, he took his two sons, Manasseh and Ephraim, to see him (Genesis 48:1). When Joseph arrived with his sons to visit his father, Jacob immediately sat up in bed. However, it was tough for Jacob to sit up in his bed because he had no energy (Genesis 48:2). Jacob told his son Joseph, "God All-Powerful appeared to me at Luz in the land of Canaan. He gave me his blessings and promised, that I will be given a large family with many descendants that will grow into a nation.

And that that land will belong to the family and me forever" (Genesis 48:3–4).

Jacob had so much to say to his son Joseph at that moment. So therefore, he continued, saying,

> Joseph, your two sons Ephraim and Manasseh were born in Egypt, but I have accepted them as my own, just like I did with your brothers Reuben and Simeon. And any children you have later will be considered yours, but their inheritance will come from Ephraim and Manasseh. But sadly, your mother, Rachel, died in Canaan after we had left northern Syria and before we reached Bethlehem. I had to bury her along the way. (Genesis 48:5–7; Joshua 13:7, 14:4)

Jacob was old and almost blind. He did not recognize Joseph's two sons, and so he asked Joseph who the boys were. Joseph replied, "They are my sons God blessed me with since I have been here in Egypt."

Jacob said, "Bring me your sons. I want to give them my blessings." So Joseph brought the boys to his father, and he hugged and kissed them. Shortly after, Jacob turned and said to Joseph, "For many years, I thought you were dead and that I would never see you again. But God has allowed me to see you and your children."

Next, Joseph noticed that his boys were near Jacob's knees and asked them to step back, and then Joseph bowed down in front of his father with his face to the ground (Genesis 48:8–12). Then Joseph got up from his father and brought his two sons next to Jacob again. Finally, Joseph led his younger son Ephraim to the left side of Jacob and his older son Manasseh to the right (Genesis 48:13).

Before Jacob blessed Joseph's two sons, he crossed his arms, putting his right hand on the head of the younger son, Ephraim, and his left hand on the head of Manasseh, the oldest son (Genesis 48:14, Matthew 19:15, Joshua 17:1). Then he gave Joseph his blessings and said, "My grandfather Abraham and my father Isaac worshiped the Lord God. He has been with me all my life. This angel has kept me safe. Now I pray that God will bless these boys and that my name and the names of Abraham and Isaac will live on because of them. I ask God to give them many children and many descendants as well" (Genesis 48:16).

Joseph disagreed with his father putting his right hand on the youngest son. Therefore, Joseph tried to move his father's right hand from Ephraim's head and place it on Manasseh (Genesis 48:17). Joseph told his father he had made a mistake by putting his right hand on the youngest son's head and not the oldest. Joseph said, "Father, you have made a mistake; this is the oldest boy, put your right hand on him" (Genesis 48:18).

Jacob responded, saying, "Son, I know what I am doing. Manasseh's family will indeed one day become a great nation. But Ephraim will be even greater than Manasseh because his descendants will become many great nations" (Genesis 48:19). Jacob told Joseph, "That in the future, the people of Israel would ask God's blessing on one another by saying, 'I pray for God to bless you as much as he blessed Ephraim and Manasseh.'" Jacob mentioned Ephraim's name first because he will be greater than Manasseh (Genesis 48:20). Lastly, Jacob told his son, Joseph, "You can see that I will not live much longer. But God will be with you and will lead you back to the land he promised our family long ago." Finally, Jacob told Joseph he was giving him the hillside he seized from the Amorites (Genesis 48:21–22 Joshua 24:32).

When Joseph went to see his father Jacob because he was sick, Jacob saw the perfect opportunity to tell him how he felt and what to expect from God. The love and faith Jacob had for God was strong. He knew God was with him, his father Isaac, and grandfather Abraham. He wanted Jacob to know. God planned Abraham's, Isaac's, Jacob's, and Joseph's lives. They are called the Patriarchs in the Bible and the ancestors of the Israelites, God's chosen people. God was with them during their trials and tribulations, and he knew they never gave up on the faith and love they had for our Lord Jesus Christ. Jacob wanted Joseph to know how his father and ancestors walked by faith and wanted him to continue to do the same. Moreover, Joseph had faith and knew God was with him when he was separated from his family.

I cannot stress enough how real God is and the love he has for us. I am a living example of what God can do when you walk by faith! God has shown me how to love everyone and not judge! Until the following letter.

Love,
Grandma

Forty-Ninth Chapter Letter

Jacob Blesses His Sons

Good afternoon, my grandkids. Today is Thursday, June 10, 2021. It is 2:00 p.m. I finished up the last letter earlier this morning, so I decided to pick it up this afternoon. In my previous letter, I shared how Jacob was sick and blessed Joseph and his two sons. He also shared how he and his father, Isaac, and grandfather, Abraham, had always worshiped God and believed he held their hands and walked with them during their lives. Jacob told Joseph about the promise God made to him at Luz and that in the future, people will ask God's blessings by saying, "I pray for God to bless you as much as he blessed Ephraim and Manasseh." When you need prayer or praying for others, I encourage you to say that prayer. It is powerful! Jacob told his son the promise God made to him to lead them back to the land he promised the family years ago.

In the following letter, I will write to you about what took place in Genesis, chapter 49. Jacob began by bringing together his twelve sons and giving each one of them his blessings. And toward the end of the chapter, Jacob died.

"Jacob called his sons together and said, 'My sons, I am Jacob, your father, Israel." He told his sons that he would tell them their future (Genesis 49:1–2, Deuteronomy 33:6, Isaiah 2:2). He started with the oldest son.

Reuben, you are my oldest born at the peak of my powers; you were an honored leader. But uncontrollable as a flood, you slept with my wife and disgraced my bed. And because of that, you no longer deserve the place of honor.

Simeon and Levi, you are brothers, each a gruesome sword. I never want to take part in your plans and deeds. You slaughtered people in your anger, and you crippled cattle for no reason. Now I place a curse on you because of your fierce anger. As a result, your descendants will be scattered among the tribe of Israel [Proverbs 1:15, Psalm 26:9, Joshua 19:1–6].

Judah, you will be praised by your brothers; they will bow down to you as you defeat your enemies. But, my son, you are a lion ready to eat your victim! You are fierce; no one will bother you. You will have power and rule until nations obey you and bring you gifts. You will tie your donkey to a choice grapevine and wash your clothes in wine from those grapes. Your eyes are darker than wine, your teeth whiter than milk [Deuteronomy 33:7, Psalm 18:40, 1 Chronicles 5:2].

Zebulun, you will settle along the seashore and provide safe harbors as far north as Sidon [Deuteronomy 33:18].

Issachar, you are a strong donkey resting in meadows. You found them so pleasant that you worked too hard and became a servant [1 Chronicles 12:32, 1 Samuel 10:9].

Dan, you are the tribe that will bring justice to Israel. You are a snake that bites the heel of a horse, making the rider fall [Deuteronomy 33:22, Judges 18:27].

Our Lord, I am waiting for you to save us [Isaiah 25:9].

Gad, you will be attacked, then attack your attackers [Deuteronomy 33:20].

Asher, you will eat food fancy enough for a king [Deuteronomy 33:24].

Naphtali, you are a wild deer with lovely fawns [Deuteronomy 33:23]!

Joseph, you are a fruitful vine growing near a stream and climbing a wall. Enemies attacked with arrows, refusing to show mercy. But you stood your ground, swiftly shooting back with the help of Jacob's God, the All-Powerful One— his name is the shepherd, Israel mighty rock [Job 29:20, Psalm 132:2, Isaiah 28:16]. Your help came from the God your father worshiped, from God All-Powerful. God will bless you with rain and streams from the earth; he will bless you with many descendants. My son, the blessings I give are better than the promise of ancient mountains or eternal hills. Joseph, I pray these blessings will come to you because you are the leader of your brothers [Deuteronomy 33:13, 35:15].

Benjamin, you are a fierce wolf destroying your enemies morning and evening [Judges
20:21]. (Genesis 49:3–27)

These were the twelve tribes of Israel, and this was how Jacob
gave each of his sons their blessings (Genesis 49:28).

Jacob's Death

After Jacob gave his sons their blessings, he said, "Soon I will
die, and I want to be buried in Machpelah Cave. My grandfather
Abraham bought this cave as a burial place from Ephron the Hittite,
and it is near the town of Mamre in Canaan. Abraham and Sarah are
buried there, and so are Isaac and Rebekah. I buried Leah there as
well" (Genesis 49:29–31). Both the cave and the land were purchased
from the Hittites (Genesis 49:32). After Jacob finished instructing
Joseph what to do, he lay down on his bed and died (Genesis 49:33).

Jacob was an incredible man. He knew every one of his son's
faults and unique skills. Therefore, Jacob told his sons what would
happen to them in the future because of their past behaviors. He outlined their faults and consequences. For example, his oldest son lost
his honored leadership role because he slept with Jacob's wife. And
Simeon and Levi were angry men who killed people, and because of
that, they will be scattered among the tribes of Israel. They would be
separated from family. And Dan would be the snake by the roadside
that "bites the heel of a horse making the rider fall." Beware of people
like him, the devil, because they are out there in the world ready to
destroy you!

On the other hand, you have Judah, the lion; his brothers will
bow down to him. He will have power, and nations will obey him
because he changed his attitude and behaviors. He showed remorse
when trying to save Benjamin. He was the only one trying to convince the governor they were innocent people, and because of that,
he was rewarded. Jesus will come from Judah's family line. Jacob
points out through his twelve sons that if you work hard and love
your neighbors as yourself, you will win. Whatever you do today

will affect your future. Stay in communication with God and build a close relationship with him, and if you have done that, you have already won because the Holy Spirit lives in us and will help you when you need help. I am going to close this letter now. It is getting late. Until the next time.

Love,
Grandma

Fiftieth Chapter Letter

Burial of Jacob

Good evening, my precious grandkids. It is June 10, 2021, and it's 8:06 p.m. Today has been a challenging day for me, dealing with Grandma Josie's mood swings. She has no filter and will curse at me when she disagrees with what I say. However, today I got my second COVID vaccine shot. After an hour, I was sleepy and tired. I'm not sure if it was from the vaccine shot. I did not have any reaction to the first shot.

Recent studies show that more than 598,000 have died in the United States because of COVID-19. I firmly believe God is in control of this virus. I think he is sending us a message. For example, in the book of Exodus, God instructed Moses to get the king of Egypt to release the Israelites from being their servants. He was holding them captive. The king refused, so God told Moses to send a disaster called the ten plagues. The king eventually released the people. We are in God's world; he created it, and he can do whatever it takes to get our attention, and it is my opinion that is what he is doing with this COVID disaster.

In the last letter, I shared how Jacob gave his sons and Joseph's two sons his blessing. Unfortunately, Joseph also told each of his sons their future, and he ended up dying. I will write about what happened in Genesis 50, the last chapter. Jacob died and was buried in Machpelah Cave as he requested his son Joseph to make sure his body would be placed there. After that, Joseph's brothers finally came

LETTERS TO MY GRANDKIDS

to him and apologized for tossing him in the well. He did not blame them and told them not to worry about it because it was God's plan for his life. Joseph dies in this chapter. He lived to be 110.

When Jacob died, Joseph started crying, held his father, and kissed him while lying in bed (Genesis 50:1). Joseph gave his servants orders to have his father's body embalmed. This process took forty days. The Egyptians mourned for seventy days. When the time was over for mourning, Joseph told the Egyptians, "Leaders, if you consider me your friend, please go ask the king to allow me to bury my father" (Genesis 50:2–4, Deuteronomy 34:8, Esther 4:2). Joseph explained to the leaders that his father wanted him to promise he would be buried in his burial cave in Canaan when he died. Joseph was hoping the king would allow him to go (Genesis 50:5). The king had no problems with Joseph's request. He said, "Go to Canaan and keep your father's promise" (Genesis 50:6).

Joseph left Goshen where his father was living. His brothers, all their relatives, and many of the king's highest officials, along with military chariots, went with Joseph to bury his father, Jacob (Genesis 50:7–9). Then they crossed the Jordan River and reached Atad's threshing place, where they all mourned and wept for seven days. The Canaanites witnessed what was going on and said, "The Egyptians are in great sorrow." And because of that, they named the place Egypt Is in Sorrow (Genesis 50:10–11, Acts 8:2).

Joseph and his brothers took their father's body to Canaan and buried him in Machpelah Cave, which their grandfather Abraham purchased from Ephron the Hittite.

Joseph's Promise to His Brothers

After their father Jacob died, the brothers said to each other, "What if Joseph still hates us and wants to get even with us for all the cruel things we did to him" (Genesis 50:15, Job 15:21)? So before their father died, he told Joseph's brothers to ask Joseph for forgiveness for all the cruel and horrible things they did to him. Thus the brothers sent their brother Joseph a message, "Now we ask you to please forgive us for the terrible things we did to you. After all, we serve the same God that your father worshiped." When Joseph heard their message, he started crying (Genesis 50:16–17, Proverbs 28:13). At that moment, these brothers came to Joseph and bowed down to the ground and said, "We are your servants."

Joseph then said, "Do not be afraid! I have no right to change what God has planned." Moreover, Joseph said, "You tried to harm me, but God made it turn out for the best so that I could save all these people, as I am doing now." Then Joseph told his brothers not to be afraid, that he would take care of them and their children. As a result, his brothers felt relieved (Genesis 50:18–21, Psalm 56:5, Matthew 5:44).

Joseph's Death

Joseph lived in Egypt with his brothers until he died at the age of 110. Joseph lived long enough to see his sons Ephraim's and Manasseh's kids and grandkids and welcomed them into the family (Genesis 50:22–23, Job 42:16, Numbers 26:29).

Joseph told his brothers he would not be living too much longer but that God would take care of them and lead them out of Egypt to the land he promised their grandfather Abraham, Isaac, and their father, Jacob (Genesis 50:24, Exodus 3:16). Moreover, Joseph instructed his brothers to take his body with them when God leads them to the promised land (Genesis 50:25). Joseph died in Egypt, and his body was embalmed (Genesis 50:26; Exodus 13:19; Deuteronomy 1:8, 30:1–8).

Genesis 50 is the last chapter in the book. After Jacob died, Joseph's brothers were afraid of what Joseph would do with them. They thought their brother would harm them or get revenge, but instead, Joseph cried after hearing their concern. Joseph did not blame them; he knew God's plan was for him to live in Egypt and save his people and the others. The brothers had a guilty conscience and were carrying that shame with them while living in Goshen. But they felt relieved once Joseph embraced and forgave them and promised he would take care of them and their families. The story was incredible, yet it depicts how God controls our lives, the world, and he will see us through troubled times. We just must believe, trust, and walk by faith as Abraham, Isaac, Jacob, and Joseph did. Now ask yourselves if you are walking by faith, and do you believe God has your back?

In Closing

The book of Genesis starts with the beginning of the universe, the human race, and the people of Israel. Adam and Eve were created, and the woman allowed the devil to ruin her family, resulting in them being kicked out of the garden! They had two sons, and one was jealous of the other and killed him, and because of that, the family was separated. Thus, family separation was a regular phenomenon in ancient times from the beginning of creation. Partly because people let the devil in, the devil manipulated and convinced people not to forgive and hold on to the grudges, which is a sin. The same is happening today in our families! The devil is happy when there is family separation and when you hold on to anger. Now ask yourselves if you are serving God or the devil.

Nothing has changed today in our world. Families continue to be angry and refuse to speak to their siblings, mother, father, and grandparents because of past hurt they are holding on to. Throughout the stories in Genesis, you read for yourselves how the families ended up separating. For example, Noah's son Ham walked into his father's tent and saw him naked and told others. Noah found out what he did and gave him consequences that led to family separation.

Abraham was called to leave his family because God had a plan for him. He left his family and married his stepsister, Sarah. Later in the story, she realized God did not bless her with a child in her old age, so she told Abraham to marry her servant Hagar who had Ishmael. And in the middle of the story, she made Hagar leave the town they were living in because she was jealous. Again, family separation!

Isaac and Rebekah had twin boys, and she favors one over the other. The older brother, Esau, got angry at his brother, Jacob, and his mother made Jacob leave town because Esau said he was going to kill him. So Rebekah, his mother, made Jacob leave town, and she never saw him again. Once more, family separation!

Jacob and his four wives had twelve sons and one daughter. The older sons became jealous of the younger brother Joseph and tossed him in a dry well, and eventually, he was sold to Potiphar, the king's official in charge of the palace. Joseph worked for Potiphar for one year and was put in prison at eighteen because he refused to have sex with his wife.

After he interpreted the king's dreams, he was made governor of Egypt at thirty years old. Joseph's brother had not seen him since he was a teenager. Then a seven-year famine came to Canaan and Egypt that forced Jacob and his sons to reach out to the governor, which turned out to be their little brother Joseph who had been separated from his family for twenty-two years!

Joseph forgave his brothers after all those years. He never held on to anger. Instead, he said it was God's will for him to live that path. So now I ask, are you holding on to past anger that separates you from your family members? If so, ask God to come into your life and cleanse your heart and help you to love people and yourself. God is real, and holding on to anger will separate you from your family, friends, husband, wife, and others, which is what the devil wants for people on this earth. Do not let the devil and sin separate you from God and the blessings he has in stored for you!

So if you find yourself stuck in anger, ask God to help you, and please use my theory on the following page and *uncover your anger one layer at a time*. In my first book called *Uncovering Anger One Layer at a Time and Learn the Power of Forgiveness*, I shared my story of being angry as a teenager and young adult. I worked with foster girls for over twenty years who were angry at their parents for not loving and caring for them. My model helped them and many others who had anger issues and wanted help. If you're angry and not speaking to your family or loved ones, I encourage you to use the four-phase model to get to the root of your anger and learn the power of forgiveness! Until the next book.

Love,
Grandma

Appendix A

Phase 1: Uncovering anger
a) Who are you angry at?
b) Are you ready to work on your anger problems?

Phase 2: Deciding to forgive
a) Can you identify the ones who hurt you?
b) Are you ready to forgive them?
c) Are you ready to forgive yourself?

Phase 3: Working on forgiveness
a) Are you ready to work on acceptance?
b) Are you ready to work on compassion?

Phase 4: Releasing the pain and anger
a) Will you take action to release the pain and anger?
b) Will you take action to communicate with the one you need to forgive?

On the following pages, on the graph, I listed the people who hurt me, starting back from childhood. The aim is to help you identify the people who hurt you and the root of where it began. The goal is to peel back the layers of your anger. For example, when my parents divorced, I was angry at my parents when I was ten years old. Secondly, I was mad because of peer pressure growing up in the inner city of San Diego; I had to fight to survive in the neighborhood. I identified all who hurt me and asked God to help me forgive them and myself. I was stuck in my anger for many years, separated from family members, friends, and had troubled relationships. Nevertheless, God helped me love myself and all people, and he will do the same for you!

Appendix B

An Example of My Layers of Built-Up Anger
I Started from the Bottom and Worked My Way Up

The last layer of anger formed
during my painting career when
I was called nigger lover.

The fifth layer of anger formed when
I was getting beat up by the
father of my children.

The fourth layer of anger formed when
I got pregnant and dropped out
of high school (I made at myself).

The third layer of anger formed when
I was a teenager and the kids in my
community called me "White girl."

The second layer of anger formed when
my parents got divorced.

The first layer of anger formed when
I was ten years old and witnessed
my parents fight.

Appendix C

Use the graph below to identify the root of your anger. Ask yourself how many layers do you have to uncover.

Bibliography

Augustine, Saint Augustine. *Nicene and Post-Nicene Fathers of the Christian Church*. Grand Rapids, Michigan: Wm. B. Eerdmans Publishing Company, 1887.

Galvez, Dr. Sylvia. *Uncovering Anger One Layer at a Time—Discover the Freedom of Forgiveness*. ISBN. 0692564764, 2015.

KJV Word Study Bible. Thomas Nelson. Library of Congress Control Number 2016939638, 2017.

Life Application Bible, New International Version. Wheaton, Illinois 60189, USA/Grand Rapids, Michigan 49506, USA: Tyndale House Publishers, Inc. and Zondervan Publishing House, 1991.

Life Application Study Bible, New Living Translation. Carol Stream. Illinois: Tyndale House Publishers, Inc., 2004.

Missler, Dr. Chuck. *Learn the Bible in 24 Hours*. Koinonia House Inc.: P.O. Box D, Coeur d'Alene, ID 83816, 2018.

The Holy Bible, Contemporary English Version. American Bible Society: 1865 Broadway, New York, NY 10023, 1997.

The Holy Bible, King James Version. Nelson Regency 991BG.

The Holy Bible, Old and New Testament in the King James. By Thomas Nelson, Inc., 1976.

The King James Study Bible, The Annotated Study Bible, King James Version. By Liberty University, 1988.

The Nelson Study Bible, New King James Version, NKJV Study Bible second Edition, 1997.

Then and Now Bible Maps Insert. Rose Publishing and Hendrickson Publishing, 2008.

The Thompson Chain-reference Bible Second Improved Edition New International Version. B.B. Kirkbride Bible Company, Inc.: Indianapolis, Indiana, 46202, USA, 1990.

Dr. Galvez grew up in southeastern San Diego, California, an angry child and teenager who would rather fight to resolve her problems. The change came when she gave her life to the Lord in her early twenties, and she's been serving him ever since. She believes family is a critical component of one's love and happiness. Dr. Galvez believes God held her hands every step of her journey. She walks by faith, loves people, and continues to believe God has her back! Dr. Sylvia Galvez is married to Herb L. Cawthorne, and together they have six kids and nineteen grandkids.

About the Author

Sylvia & Herb

Dr. Sylvia Galvez dropped out of high school, became a single mother at sixteen, and had two more sons when she turned twenty-one. Knowing she had to make a living, she entered the construction field as a painter. Never satisfied, Dr. Galvez returned to school at age twenty-eight. She earned her AA, BA, masters, and a doctorate in educational leadership while working full time and providing for her young boys.

For twenty years, Dr. Galvez owned and operated state-licensed residential group homes for foster girls who had been abused and abandoned. Through her nonprofit organization, Dr. Galvez dedicated her life to foster girls and their families by systematically helping them uncover their anger one layer at a time. Dr. Sylvia Galvez currently counsels teenagers, young adults, and families on how to overcome their anger, past hurt, and pain through the word of God. She believes in the power of love and forgiveness.